BLACK BELT
P R E S E N T S

STAY in the FIGHT

A Martial Athlete's Guide to Preventing and Overcoming Injury

Danny Dring and Johnny D. Taylor

Copyright © 2010 Cruz Bay Publishing, Inc
First Printing 2010
All Rights Reserved
Printed in South Korea

Library of Congress Number: 2010934974
ISBN-10: 0-89750-187-X
ISBN-13: 978-0-89750-187-3

Edited by Sarah Dzida, Allison Arbuthnot and Cassandra Harris
Cover and graphic design by John Bodine

For information about permission to reproduce selection from this book,
write Black Belt Books, 24900 Anza Dr. Unit E Valencia, CA. 91355

For information about bulk/wholesale purchases, please contact 1 (800) 423-2874 ext. 1633

BLACK BELT BOOKS
A Division of **OHARA** PUBLICATIONS, INC.
World Leader in Martial Arts Publications

ABOUT THE AUTHORS

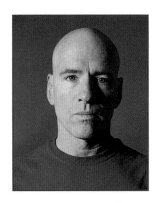

Danny Dring *Black Belt* contributor Danny Dring holds a seventh-degree degree black belt in *taekwondo*, *jujutsu* and Bill Wallace's Fighting System, a sixth-degree black belt in Joe Lewis Fighting Systems, and a third-degree black belt in Brazilian *jiu-jitsu*.

As a competitor, Dring's career highlights include six international gold medals and two international silver medals in taekwondo. He is a four-time national circuit champion for the United States Taekwondo Federation and a five-time open-circuit state champion. As a kickboxer, Dring had a winning record, and he also competed once on ESPN's Professional Karate Association TV series.

As a coach, Dring has produced world champions and professional fighters in kickboxing and mixed martial arts. He has actively promoted kickboxing and MMA events. He also has served on the Arkansas State Athletic Commission (the boxing, kickboxing and MMA regulatory body) as a commissioner. Dring is a certified defensive-tactics instructor and certified pistol instructor in Arkansas. He has served as a reserve deputy for the Pulaski County Sheriff's Office since 1993. He owns and operates Living Defense Martial Arts. For more information about Dring, visit www.livingdefense.com.

Johnny D. Taylor has been involved in martial arts for seven years and holds a second-degree black belt in taekwondo as well as a blue belt in Brazilian jiu-jitsu under Danny Dring's school of Living Defense Martial Arts. He teaches fundamental martial arts and fitness, emphasizing character development as well as physical prowess. He is a contributing writer for *Black Belt* and has been a Christian minister for over 25 years.

STAY in the FIGHT

A Martial Athlete's Guide to Preventing and Overcoming Injury

Danny Dring and Johnny D. Taylor

TABLE OF CONTENTS

PREFACE

As fighters, we know injury, but we don't always know what to do with it. We need practical instruction and inspiring motivation to give us confidence and direction in order to deal with our injuries and continue our martial arts lifestyles. Most of all we need hope that we aren't forever sidelined, and we need to be given that hope by people who understand firsthand what it means to be an injured fighter. Unlike other books by sports medicine professionals, this book is presented from the perspective of the martial artist, from personal experience and from the heart of the warrior athlete.

Whether you are dealing with injury that is severe or mild, wanting to avoid injury as you train or dealing with the inevitable effects of aging, we want to see your martial life extended and enhanced. We hope that through the work of this book you will be well-equipped, fired up and ready to be proactive, go on the offensive and attack your unacceptable circumstances with the same heart and zeal that made you a martial artist in the first place.

In over 30 years of martial arts competitions, training and school operations, Danny Dring has seen and experienced a constant procession of injuries but found little in the way of an organized or well-rounded methodology for treating athletes and getting them back to the training they love. As a martial artist and writer, Johnny Taylor also knows the struggle of injury recovery, the myriad of questions that an injury brings and the difficulty of finding a good source for solutions. After an experimental hip-resurfacing procedure enabled Mr. Dring to return to hard-core training, he began to receive correspondence and emails from injured people all around the country and he found that he was not alone. Their chief concern: Is there any hope for me to return to athleticism?

Together, we realized that between our own personal experience in both physical and mental conditioning and with Mr. Dring's array of high-caliber contacts in the martial arts world, we had the makings for a much needed and very helpful book. The prospect of helping thousands of martial athletes extend their career, whether professional or amateur, excited us very much.

We wanted a book that was more than lecture and more than how-to exercises. We wanted to offer our readers a comprehensive, actionable strategy that they could apply and work through to see real results in athleticism and wellness.

Through a series of long interviews and discussions about the various topics covered in this book, Mr. Dring's personal philosophy and experiences in the area of injury and recovery were gathered. We also sought out the most qualified professionals we had access to through Mr. Dring's friends and colleagues. Through further interviews, we gathered the best wisdom of martial arts legends Joe Lewis and Bill Wallace, Brazilian *jiu-jitsu* superstar Robson Moura, Renegade Coach John Davies, Dr. David Klein, former National Association of Professional Martial Artists curriculum coordinator Mark Graden and sports therapist Mark Young. These extremely knowledgeable men graciously gave us the benefit of not only their expertise but also their own personal stories of injury and recovery. We are grateful for their willingness to enrich the book and the reader's experience.

As a result, we have done our best to bring about a volume that not only informs but inspires, motivates and moves the reader to instant, beneficial action through a customized plan of execution. The material is arranged in chronological order from initial injury to fullest possible recovery, first dealing with the physical aspects and then the mental disciplines necessary for optimal health and athleticism. As you work your way through the book, it is important that your study include all areas covered and that you complete the "Fightsheet" work pages included for each chapter. They comprise your personalized action plan for your own return to maximized martial athleticism. We have also included sidebars, graphics, quotes and other special features to not only add interest and further information, but to keep you inspired and motivated in your journey. We know that having facts and procedures is never enough for a martial athlete. Driven by heart, desire and a fighting spirit, our martial philosophy enables us to thrive on higher ideals and a deeper sense of purpose.

So it is with a sense of gratitude that we offer this book. Our sincere thanks to the professionals mentioned above for their graciousness, to Black Belt Books, and to our editor Sarah Dzida for helping to turn our idea into reality.

May we all stay in the fight.

—Danny Dring
Johnny D. Taylor
2010

CHAPTER ONE
THE FIGHT OF YOUR LIFE

It's fight day! You want to test your mettle so you sign up.
You find out that you will be facing a particularly mean and nasty opponent.
The stakes are high and you know you can expect a very tough fight,
maybe the fight of your life. This is what the draw has put in front of you,
and you are ready.

"Injured ... "

"Sidelined ... "

"Too old ... "

"You'll never be able to fight again ... "

These are phrases that put a cold knot of dread in the stomach of the martial athlete, filling the mind with thoughts and images of loss and even fear. Yet all too often they define the reality of the martial arts life.

From the professional MMA cage fighter to the white belted "little dragon," from the soldier in the field to the security guard and the housewife in a *taekwondo* class, the martial arts hold not only the broad appeal of an active lifestyle but the possibility, even probability, of injury. As a martial artist, you know that you are not immune to injury, but that every time you practice your art, you run the risk of being hurt. After all, the very nature of the martial arts is to inflict pain and injury. If nobody gets kicked, punched, torqued, or thrown, is it really "martial?" So you can expect that sooner or later, one way or another, you will probably suffer injury. Add to that the martial attitude of intensity along with the never-ending pursuit of advancement that spur the athlete to push the envelope of personal safety, and you can see why injury is an integral part of the martial arts lifestyle. So martial athletes like ourselves should simply expect that we will always be addressing some physical issue, that we will get injured, that we will need to recover and that we will need to get back to training.

It may be that the very reason you are reading this book is because you are currently dealing with an injury, whether martial arts related or not. Perhaps you were in the middle of preparing for an event when injury struck. Perhaps you are dealing with a major life-altering situation. You are finding that your fight against injury is the fight of your life, and you are wondering if there is anything you can do to get going athletically again. Maybe your injury is relatively mild, but you worry it may get worse and you need to heal properly and permanently.

Now, it is true that you have the option to simply quit, do nothing and try to heal as best you can. But if you do, you may never achieve maximized healing of the body. Worse, injuries can take on a deeper, internal nature in your mind, changing your image of yourself from that of a fighter to that of a weak victim. That mind-set can keep you weakened and wounded for life.

Graph Showing Athletic Prehab's Place in Martial Arts Athleticism Recovery

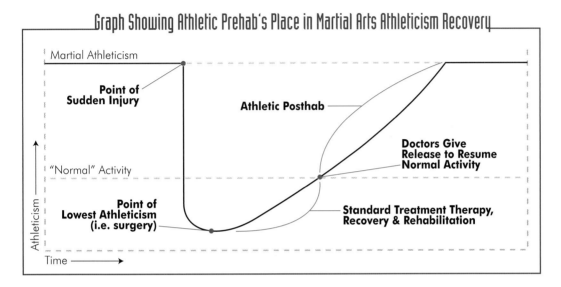

Injury prevention may also be a great concern for you. You may be getting into the martial arts for the first time or returning after several years of a sedentary lifestyle. There is also the opponent of aging that robs us of athleticism and vigor. At any rate, you need to know how to prepare your body for martial athletic requirements such as twisting, punching and kicking. An injury prevented is better than an injury overcome.

No matter your situation, you may be asking yourself such questions as:

- Can I recover from my injury?
- What is the quickest route to the fullest possible recovery?
- To what degree will I be able to continue my martial arts?
- What specifically can I do for my injury?
- What beneficial activities can I be doing while my body heals?
- How can I avoid injury while building athleticism?

The good news is that there *are* answers to your questions, and you *don't* have to just lie down and quit. The road to your own optimized health and wellness may be neither short nor easy, but it is open to you. Consider that there are many people in the world who have suffered from injuries similar to your own. If any one of them has been able to regain their athleticism and come back, then so can you. Plus, you're a martial athlete! So if anyone can do it, you can.

To that end, we, the authors, will help you navigate the sometimes confusing pathways of a wide range of health and recovery issues as they pertain to martial artists. These topics include:

- how to reverse muscle atrophy and take a recovered injury back to optimum athleticism
- how to choose the proper medical professionals
- where to find information on your injury and methods of treatment
- how to work around an injury
- specific exercises for common martial arts injuries
- how to set and achieve goals for injury recovery
- how to master the emotional rollercoaster that often comes with injury
- the best ways to stay occupied during your down time
- nutritional concerns
- keeping a positive attitude
- developing the persistence and patience to see your recovery through to the end
- how to deal with the inevitable aging process

In addition, we've striven to provide the four necessary ingredients of any good training program:

- **Inspiration:** descriptions of what is possible for a human being to accomplish.
- **Motivation:** the belief in all that is possible for you to accomplish.
- **Education:** how to accomplish your recovery goals and reach your potential.
- **Activation:** clear direction on what to do and encouragement to complete the task at hand.

The information in this book contains wisdom gleaned from years of personal and professional experience, presented not only from us authors but also from a wide range of martial athletes and medical professionals. It is our intention to put these exceptional professionals in your "corner." They will give you the benefit of their vast knowledge, decades of experience, personal philosophies, and tried and true methodology to help you attain optimal health and wellness as a martial artist regardless of your age, background or situation.

In this book, you will hear from martial arts legends such as Joe Lewis, Bill Wallace and seven-time world BJJ champion Robson Moura. You will hear from professionals like athletic trainer John Davies, medical practitioner Dr. David Klein, sports therapist Mark Young and former National Association of Professional Martial Artists curriculum coordinator Mark Graden.

Book co-author Danny Dring offers the benefit of his philosophy and experience, too. In over 30 years in the martial arts, he has been the student, teacher, coach, trainer, promoter, amateur and professional. He has experienced injury to practically every part of his body and knows firsthand what it means to come back and to stay in the fight. (At the time of this writing, he is running bleachers as part of his training regimen—even with an artificial hip.)

The book's other author, Johnny Taylor, is a second-degree black belt from Danny Dring's school, a teacher and writer with a particular understanding of martial principles in the areas of mind and spirit. He also brings the wisdom gleaned from his own experiences of injury and healing as a nonprofessional lifestyle martial artist.

These martial artists and medical and athletic professionals will share their stories. Many have been exactly where you may be today, and they will tell you from personal experience what to expect, what is possible, and how they made their own comeback. As they share their own unique experiences with injury and what they were able to accomplish after their recovery, it is hoped that you will see them as living proof of what you are able to do as well.

Another major goal of this book is to give you a road map to follow and guide you each step of the way. This book will provide you with a personalized plan and the tools, knowledge and encouragement that you need to make the best of your own journey from injury to recovery.

Each chapter has its own work pages called a "Fightsheet" for you to fill out as it pertains to you and your particular situation. They will help you ask and answer the right questions to address your own specific needs. By carefully and diligently completing each Fightsheet, you will not only gain insights into your own particular situation, but you will build a customized training program to carry you through the whole process from pre-injury to maximum recovery. These Fightsheets will help you determine your best course of action and put together a plan for issues such as:

- workout routines for many common martial arts injuries
- dealing with pain
- range of motion and warm-up routines
- optimal diet and recommended supplements for best recovery
- planning your martial arts future
- overcoming depression

You'll find Fightsheets for each chapter at the end of book in their own section. (See page 125.) Therefore, it is important that you complete this book, otherwise you won't have a complete plan, and you may fall short of achieving your optimal health, recovery and athleticism.

So with all of that said, are you ready? Are you ready?

Fight!

When I had my hip replaced I was told I would probably have to give it all up. After rupturing my bicep tendon I was told I wouldn't be able to punch anymore. So far, I've proven all those people wrong.

I worked hard for years to develop my flexibility only to see it go from "freaky flexible" to "limited mobility" in the hip. It didn't happen overnight but it was a long, slow process. I lost a little range of motion here, had a little more pain there and found that my hip problems began to creep into my whole martial arts life. I wasn't doing the things I used to do: walking the dog or going out with my kids and family, because of the pain. I forced myself to do some training but then would have to go sit down.

I was eventually diagnosed with necrosis of the hip; in other words, the ball of my hip joint was dying. I had a core decompression, meaning they drilled into the

Photo courtesy of Danny Dring

ball of the hip in an attempt to get it to revascularize—grow new living tissue and blood vessels. This was all done to try to bring life back to the dead bone in my hip. That bought me some time, but the pain still kept getting worse and worse. Again, it wasn't anything dramatic, but one day I realized my very lifestyle had changed. I wasn't doing the things that I really wanted to do.

So I did my research. I learned about the hip, vascular necrosis, other available options, who was doing what, and where the groundbreaking procedures were being done. I didn't want to get a typical artificial hip and lose my ability to play martial arts. I eventually discovered a prosthesis company and surgeons that I wanted to use. I had the metal-on-metal hip resurfacing surgery for the Wright Medical Conserve Plus.

I've been thrilled with the results. I eventually got back into a full center split. I am able to run, jump, kick and do everything I used to do. There are a few parameters for me, but they are very minor compared with what I stood to lose without the proper course of action. It really is amazing what modern medicine can do. When you couple modern medicine with the age-old disciplines and attitudes that are integral to martial-athletic life, you will find that there has never been a better time to overcome injury.

CHAPTER TWO
THE SIX DIMENSIONS OF ATHLETIC HEALTH

In the ring, you are ready for round one. You mentally go over your strategy. You have trained hard and you know what you are capable of. You know your strengths, best techniques and how to maximize them. You know your weight is right, hydration level is good and there is plenty of "gas in your tank." You know that you are ready. The ref yells, "FIGHT!" You go to work. Not only are muscles and bones engaged, but so are breathing, agility, coordination and balance as you throw your whole being into the fight.

Holism is the idea that the whole is more than just the sum of its parts. A classic automobile for example is more than just a collection of mechanical parts, and a martial athlete is more than just legs, arms, torso, head and skills. That means whatever strength provided by one part benefits the whole, and whatever affects one part affects the whole. Holism is one of the underlying principles of life, and it is the approach used throughout this book in dealing with injury, recovery, health and wellness.

Unfortunately, an injury is also holistic in nature. More than just an area of damaged tissue, it can have far-reaching effects and can seem to take on a life of its own. Since you are more than a collection of parts, what affects one part of your body affects other parts as well. An injured shoulder is not just an injured shoulder, for instance. Instead, it results in an injured athlete with deficits in many areas of athletic health such as strength and range of motion. Just as it is impossible to isolate the injured shoulder from your arm or back, so it is impossible to isolate the negative effects of an injury. An injured toe makes your whole body walk with a limp. Infection can spread. Time in a cast can cause atrophy to an entire limb. Resources necessary for healing a localized injury can mean fewer resources available to the rest of the body.

That is why you need a holistic plan for injury recovery, one that addresses the many dimensions of athletic health. If your thinking, actions and planning are holistic in nature, the various elements of your plan will all work together, bring additional benefits and turn dealing with a specific injury into extraordinary recovery and accomplishment for the whole athlete. By addressing all the dimensions of athletic health, you may be able to come out of injury stronger in some ways then when you went in. This is how you can make the most of the recovery challenge.

As we begin our holistic journey to optimal recovery, health and wellness for the whole martial artist, we will start with the athlete's body and understanding its many needs and complexities. To do so, we must understand and address the six dimensions of athletic health and seek to build up all of them together.

Like spokes in a wheel, the six dimensions of athletic health—strength, cardio (cardio-respiratory endurance), flexibility, nutrition, hydration and rest—are not only important individually but are necessary to lend stability to the whole. All are required to be in good shape in order for forward movement to be possible. A wheel, after all, is more than the sum of its parts.

SIX DIMENSIONS OF ATHLETIC HEALTH

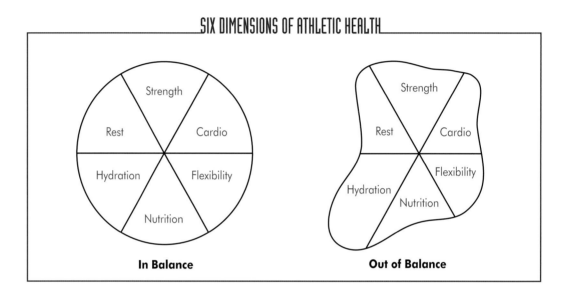

In Balance   **Out of Balance**

STRENGTH

Your ability to throw a punch, hold a kick, take down a grappling opponent, escape a hold, and any number of other skills depends on the proper function of your musculature and sufficient power. This means that there is no substitute for strength training in the martial arts. So in terms of overall health and injury prevention, strength training can result in a body that is less prone to injury. After all, a strong limb isn't as easily injured as a weak one.

For the injured athlete, strength training is often an integral part of the recovery process.

If you are facing surgery, having a strengthened and well-muscled area surrounding the incision site can speed recovery time. It can also prevent some of the post-surgery atrophy that will result from prolonged disuse and immobilization of the injured body part.

However, rather than thinking of strength as a function of muscles only, consider that there are many physical systems and components involved in the act of exercising physical power. Consider all the tendons, bones, ligaments, cartilages, blood vessels, nerves and more that are involved when physical strength is exercised. Consider also the necessary blood flow to all involved tissues, the complex activity of your nervous system, and how your respiratory and endocrine systems are brought into play. So think about all the parts involved when you strength-train your muscles—you will also be strengthening all those above mentioned tissues and systems so that the benefits are many and varied.

Benefits from strength training include:

- increased bone density
- stronger ligaments and tendons
- improved blood pressure
- improved posture
- higher metabolic rate and more energy
- improved blood circulation and lower resting heart rate
- fighting the aging process by maintaining muscle mass
- higher testosterone levels
- of course, more physical strength

From Your Corner:
Bill "Superfoot" Wallace

If you need a new joint, surgery, or other serious procedure, then go ahead and get it done. If you don't, other things are going to go bad. You'll overcompensate for one knee with the other knee, the lumbar, or the other hip. You'll start walking differently, and it will affect your whole body. So do it before the muscles, tendons, ligaments and everything else around that joint start to atrophy. You need all your surrounding tissues to be strong so you can recover more quickly and completely.

CARDIO (CARDIO-RESPIRATORY ENDURANCE)

As every martial artist knows, a good workout, sparring session or fight can leave you out of breath and exhausted. On the other hand, still having energy to continue when an opponent or partner is breathing hard and losing power gives you a decided edge.

Cardiovascular health is the body's ability to transport and use oxygen, and your stamina when breathing hard is a function of your cardio health. The heart, lungs, blood vessels and blood deliver oxygen to the muscles and other tissues to keep them operating. The better your cardio health is, the longer your athletic endurance and the shorter your recovery time will be, because without the efficient delivery of oxygen, things shut down. Just witness a BJJ or MMA choke, and you'll see just how fast the lack of oxygen can render a fighter unconscious.

When you are injured, perhaps one of the first athletic abilities to go is your cardio, since most cardio exercises consist of full-body movements. It is difficult to run, spar, do drill work or other cardio-strengthening exercises with an injury. But for the injured athlete, the need for cardio endurance is still vitally important. After all, if healthy tissues are so dependent on proper oxygenation, how much more so are tissues that are in need of rebuilding and repair?

Turning our attention to the holistic nature of this important dimension, we can see that aspects such as strength and stamina are affected by cardio health. Also consider that without proper oxygenation through the cardio-respiratory process, nutrition can become ineffective because fuel can't be "burned" without oxygen. Even flexibility training is affected by oxygen or the lack thereof. For example, consider a strained back muscle. When you hold a stretch such as touching your toes for a long period of time, the blood flow to those muscles is restricted—blood supplies are squeezed out of the tissues and muscle fibers deprived of oxygen are weakened. Using those same oxygen-starved muscles to pull yourself out of the stretch can result in strains and tears in the muscle fibers. To avoid this injury, raise yourself up out of the stretch with your spine and legs by bending your knees, tucking your pelvis, and slowly raising up. (See Figure 1.) This prevents added strain on oxygen depleted back muscles and allows them to regain blood and oxygen flow before you need to engage them again.

Figure 1

1-4: To avoid straining your back, bend your knees, tuck your pelvis and slowly raise up with your chest lifted high.

Because cardio is important to athletic health, anything you can do to get your breathing and heart rate up is good. For instance, if your injury is to the upper body, try a stationary bike. If you have an issue with a leg, try a rowing machine, dumbbell work or even swimming if possible. A circuit training routine can be designed with a little creativity that will offer sufficient exercise to improve cardio health.

The benefits of cardio go beyond the obvious of the ability to fight harder and longer. There are many other, perhaps less obvious benefits that make cardio training a needed part of the martial artist's regimen, whether injured or not.

- sufficient oxygenation of all tissues throughout the body
- the ability to burn off unwanted fat
- heart health that translates into lowered risk for heart attack
- lower blood pressure
- improved cholesterol levels
- increased metabolism and energy
- shorter recovery time after workouts as increased blood flow not only pumps oxygen and nutrients in, but waste products out
- improved hormone levels including endorphins, the "feel good" compounds released during a cardio workout
- helps to control type 2 diabetes by increasing sucrose metabolism

FLEXIBILITY

Flexibility, also known as range of motion, is a very important dimension of athletic health, especially for the martial artist. After all, what discipline puts more emphasis on dynamic flexibility than the martial disciplines? The ability to kick high still stands as a trademark move for many martial arts styles, and it is only by virtue of sufficient flexibility that many moves can be executed properly. In addition, a flexible joint will bend more, meaning that you'll be less likely to injure it.

How important is flexibility training to the recovery of the injured athlete? Very. Your doctor may very well recommend seeing a physical therapist as part of your rehabilitation protocol and you can be certain you're going to be doing a great deal of range-of-motion exercises. These medical professionals know that returning to optimal functioning means recovering range of motion that may have been lost through injury, swelling, disuse and the build up of scar tissue which must be reorganized and integrated into the surrounding tissues in order for the injured area to work properly. When the physical therapy sessions have ceased and you have been cleared to return to the gym, be sure to continue regaining and improving your range of motion.

For a recovering injury, proper, gentle stretching can increase strength and circulation as well as prevent further loss of motion and hasten healing. Other benefits of stretching as part of an injury recovery regimen include reduction of stiffness of injured joints, and the fact that the motions of stretching help to pump the fluids of

The body is complicated, and every element needs other elements to support it. For instance, a broken bone needs calcium to repair bone tissue, but it also needs vitamin D to assist in the metabolic uptake of dietary calcium so that it can be used to heal the bone.

swelling out of affected tissues and pump oxygenated blood into them. (Caution: A good rule of thumb is no stretching for the first 72 hours after an injury. You need to let some of the swelling go down first, and even then you may need to consult a qualified medical professional.)

Here is a list of some of the benefits of well-developed flexibility:

- high kicks, of course
- improved performance in other moves due to greater range of motion
- fewer pulled muscles
- fewer "turned" ankles and other joints
- restretching and lengthening of muscles and limbs that are often held close and tight during a workout such as boxing or ground fighting
- resulting grace of movement from long, supple muscles
- improved postural alignment
- the ability to get out of tight spots such as chokes, armbars, mounts and guard ground positions
- prevention or reversal of loss of flexibility that results from poor healing, aging or arthritis

NUTRITION

Your body is made up many parts—internal organs, muscles, the skeleton and other complicated systems. In turn, those pieces of anatomy are made up of tissues that perform certain functions. Muscles contract, bone marrow produces blood, adrenal glands produce adrenaline, and on and on it goes. All those many types of tissues are made of complex, living cells and every one of them needs food in order to stay alive and perform their functions. You are an amazing, almost infinitely complex creation, and every iota of you has a need to feed. So whether you are punching, kicking, grappling, swinging a sword, warming up, cooling down, building mass or losing fat, everything runs on fuel and that fuel is your nutrition.

Genuine health begins at the cellular level, and healthy cells require good nutrition.

Your body needs macronutrients such as proteins, carbohydrates and fats, and micronutrients such as vitamins and minerals in order to be in optimal health.

In times of injury and recovery, proper nutrition plays an even more important role. If healthy tissues and cells require

Starches and simple carbohydrates don't curb your appetite. That's why you can eat a ton of them when you have the "munchies" and still be hungry. You need protein and fat to turn off the feelings of hunger. This is one of the reasons why a low-fat diet is difficult for some people: They are hungry all the time.

good nutrition to recover from a regular workout, how much more do injured tissues and cells need in order to mend and recover?

When injury occurs (and the same goes for surgery), the affected area sends out a call for help to the whole body. Much of the body's resources are focused on repair and recovery, and often the demand is great. In short, injury takes a lot out of you to repair, rebuild and bring you to health and soundness, and the materials for all this construction are in the elements of your nutrition. In order to heal properly, you need to eat properly.

Worlds of information are constantly being written on the subject of nutrition, but here is a brief list of some benefits of proper nutrition for the martial athlete:

- good health for all cells, tissues, organs and overall body
- longer life
- body composition and weight management
- control of type 2 diabetes, blood pressure, heart health, cholesterol and hormones
- better resistance to sickness and disease
- slowing of the aging process
- better ability to perform your martial art using well fed muscles, bones and brains

From Your Corner:
**Renegade Coach
John Davies**

For athletes training seriously and looking for above-average gains in muscle mass and repair, I would make the following suggestions, based upon a 200-pound athlete on the proper use of BCAA (branched-chain amino acids, measured in grams):

- **Non-training days:** 2.5 grams, 3-4 times per day
- **Training days:** 5 grams upon waking; 2.5 grams 90 minutes prior to working out; 5 grams at start of workout; 5 grams prior to sleep.

HYDRATION

Your body is 70 percent water, and water is necessary for all life. Water transports nutrients, oxygen, waste products, hormones and an astounding array of other chemical and biological compounds. It regulates the processes and chemical reactions in every living cell. Water is the matrix through which electric impulses travel throughout the body. Water cools you through evaporation and warms you by transferring metabolic body heat. It provides form and structure to cells and eyeballs, thins or thickens your blood as needed and cushions your brain.

Water is life.

During a workout, your body can absorb about 24 to 32 ounces of water in an hour. However, one problem is that in hot weather you may lose twice that amount during a strenuous workout. Dehydration can also be an accumulated effect over more than one day. Also, as you sweat, you lose not only water but also minerals such as sodium, chloride and magnesium. You also burn carbohydrates, which must be replaced to maintain energy. So it is even more important to make sure that you are drinking ample amounts of fluid. A rule of thumb is to drink water for workouts that last under an hour, and perhaps a "sports drink" for longer workouts.

For the martial athlete, proper hydration is as necessary to the execution of martial endeavors as nutrition or cardio endurance, perhaps even more so since nutrition and oxygen are delivered via water. It is important to replace lost water during a workout to maintain proper hydration levels. Heavy exercise can cause a martial athlete to lose up to a gallon of water an hour through perspiration. The loss of water has a serious effect on the body's ability to perform.

So monitor your hydration level carefully. One way is to weigh yourself before and after a workout. Most of the weight loss is water so replace it as you lose it. Also, don't count on thirst to tell your body when you need more water. Exercise tends to suppress the thirst response, so by the time you feel thirsty, you are already mildly dehydrated. Consider again that if proper hydration is so vital to the health and wellness of a completely sound athlete, of how much more importance is it for injury recovery and healing?

Extra nutrients, oxygen and biochemicals are needed, as are additional blood flow and waste removal. Water is again the medium by which all this and more will occur.

Remember too that when you are recovering and your volume of exercise is decreased, you may have a tendency to drink less water. Your habitual bottles of water after a workout are no longer consumed which may mean lower hydration levels. Also, you may be tempted to drink more of other liquids such as alcohol or caffeinated beverages. These are diuretic substances and may wring more water out of your tissues at a time when it is most needed.

Keep your "body of water" well supplied with ample amounts of clean, life-giving water. Proper water levels in your

Affects of Dehydration on Athleticism

- Lose one to two percent of your body weight in water, and you will have an increase in core temperature.

- Lose three percent and the temperature increase is significant.

- Lose five percent and you will have a definite decrease in cardio (aerobic) ability and muscular endurance, possibly 20 to 30 percent decrease in strength, and be susceptible to heat exhaustion.

- At six percent loss, expect muscle spasms and cramping.

- Lose 10 percent or more of your body weight in water, and you are in danger of heat stroke and circulatory collapse.

systems will mean:

- greater endurance and strength
- better movement of resources within your body
- proper blood viscosity and nervous system operation
- fewer strained muscles since dry tissues are less flexible than well-hydrated ones

REST

Rest is one of those dimensions that people know about but don't practice often. Common sense tells us that we need to take the stress off our body so it can relax, rest and repair itself. The far-reaching effects of not getting enough sleep are still being discovered, and our own experiences remind us that a lack of sleep adversely affects us not only physically but mentally as well. Therefore, a tired and sleepy martial artist simply will not be as effective as one who is well rested.

You need serious rest to replenish depleted resources for the body, mind and spirit. Let's take the example of the human growth hormone, which is released when you sleep. HGH is used by the body to facilitate important healing processes like: cell

replacement, conversion of body fat to muscle mass, tissue growth, bone strength, brain function, enzyme production and increased energy levels. So if you rest well, you will have helped your body and your next practice out a lot.

Now let's take the example of another hormone known as cortisol. A lack of sleep produces excess amounts on this hormone, which impedes your ability to break down fat, creates blood sugar imbalances, slows healing and assists in the storage of fat around your midsection.

A good workout, especially a weight-resistance routine, results in muscle tissue breakdown, the depletion of glycogen (muscle

Those who chronically get less sleep than they need tend to store more body fat and their cortisol levels increase. Proper rest becomes even more important in the fight against declining athleticism.

"fuel") and depletion of water. The "body building" process occurs during times of rest.

For the martial athlete recovering from an injury, you only have to listen to the doctor's advice to understand the importance of rest. Simply resting the affected area is not enough; you need proper sleep for proper healing. There is much healing that will only occur while the body is asleep.

Benefits of proper rest for the martial athlete are many:

- Cell and tissue repair can progress unhindered when you are resting.

- While you rest and sleep, digestion makes nutrients available through the bloodstream to all the living cells of your body.
- Important chemicals for your brain are replenished while you rest.
- Your subconscious mind has time to sort through and deal with the massive amounts of stimuli you receive on a daily basis. It needs the "conscious you" to be out of the way so it can work. The resulting understanding from the subconscious mind becomes part of your personal knowledge, and so you learn.
- A sleep-deprived martial artist is more prone to accidents, mishaps, misunderstandings and a generally poor performance, both physically and mentally.

FOR THE MATURING MARTIAL ARTIST

As you age, you become more prone to injury and can expect longer healing and recovery times. Recuperation from workouts takes longer. Hormone levels, including testosterone and growth hormone, decrease. There is a cumulative effect of years of wear and tear on the body, resulting in an overall decline of athleticism and vigor. Elasticity of the skin and other organs of the body is lost due to reduced levels of collagen and elastin, resulting in wrinkles and sagging. The body seems to be better at laying down calcium than connective tissue. This means that ligaments, tendons, joints and other tissues can become calcified, which results in stiffness, pain and loss of flexibility. Percentage of lean muscle mass goes down and percentage of body fat goes up. Arthritis, bursitis, balding, loss of vision and hearing, loss of bone density, loss of disc material in the spinal column, incontinence, brain shrinkage, erectile dysfunction, scar tissue buildup ... and after all that, let's add depression!

Let's face it, if you ignore the passing of time and pretend to be young forever, you will one day find that age has done its work anyway. On the other hand, if you face this opponent squarely and with a good game plan, you can find that there are actually benefits that come with age.

When it comes to your game plan, extra attention needs to be given to the six dimensions of health. In regards to strength, a mature martial artist needs to be a bit more careful when lifting weight because of increased risk of injury. At the same time, strength training will help the mature martial artist maintain lean muscle mass and bone density, among other benefits. Just make sure all your workouts aren't killers. Also, the more "miles" you put on the body, the more extra care must be given to properly warming up, cooling down, icing and post-workout stretching.

Getting your heart rate up for at least 30 minutes three times a week is another good rule of thumb. By maintaining your aerobic endurance through cardio health, you'll lower your risk of heart attack, stroke and respiratory disease. Other benefits include lower blood pressure, stress relief and an increase in mood-elevating chemicals such as endorphins.

Because natural aging processes include calcification, bone loss and overall "stiffness," a continued regimen of flexibility exercises can be very valuable in maintaining your hard fought gains in flexibility. Even the effects of arthritis may be held somewhat at bay by maintaining flexibility training. Also, accidental falls account for many injuries and even deaths. When it comes to the body, it's better to be able to bend than to break.

For that same reason, physical balance is also important. In the martial arts, there is much balance training in conjunction with working for greater flexibility. Not only is stretching done in a "passive" way where you pull your body into a stretch and relax (such as "splits"), but also in "active" stretching where you use a limb's own muscles to pull itself into a more dynamic stretch (such as the slow kicks in a *kata*). This kind of flexibility training coupled with balance can go a long way in preventing falls and other accidents.

If proper nutrition and hydration is important to a young and resilient athlete, how much more important is it for athletes who've logged a lot of years, miles and injuries? Even mild dehydration can increase the danger of straining and tearing tissues. It only stands to reason that an "old and worn" joint may need a little extra lubricating and hydrating to perform at its best and also to minimize additional wear and tear.

As age increases, so may the need for quality rest in order to properly recover and recuperate from workouts and other strenuous activities. There is much healing and restoration that only occurs while we sleep. Since an older athlete needs all the healing and restoration possible, getting our rest becomes even more important as the years go by.

Proper rest is also good for your overall mental attitude. Sleep can act as a great way to dump excess stress. It can also give your mind time to sort through the overwhelming amount of stimuli we are bombarded with on a daily basis. So, while you once may have been able to go hard-charging through your days on four to six hours of sleep each night, don't be surprised to find that as you age, you will begin to need seven or eight. Otherwise you may feel worn out, find it more difficult to maintain mental focus, notice a loss in technical ability, and seem to catch every cold, illness and "ick" that comes along.

On a brighter note, with age comes experience. In fact, the title of "master" is reserved for those who have put in their years and gained uncommon experience. The sheer volume of experiences that a martial artist amasses over many years can serve to enrich a person's life in ways that nothing else can. Experience can build the ability to keep a cool head under pressure. It can also build a confidence and courage based on expert knowledge of martial technique and the inner convictions that are established over time. Years of experience can also result in special abilities such as pain tolerance, extreme body control, energy transfer and that sixth sense that enables the master to be aware of things that are often missed by the young.

From Your Corner:
Joe Lewis

As you get older, in your late 30s, say, you start losing some of your stamina. You just can't hang in there for those twenty rounds anymore, and you can't run that six to eight miles every day and still fight.

In your 40s, you start losing your eyesight and other things, and recuperative time is noticeably longer.

In your 20s, you can do a hard workout, and go right back and do it again.

In your 30s, you need twelve hours to recuperate.

In your 40s, you need a day or day and a half.

And in your 50s and 60s, you need three days to recuperate from the same workout.

So the older you get, the more you have to pace yourself. Some ways to do that are to not work out as hard or alternate between a hard workout one day, take the next day off and do a light workout the next day, getting in three workouts per week.

That's true whether you are hitting the weights, or the bag, or whatever.

From Your Corner:
Danny Dring

When you see guys like Joe Lewis, Bill Wallace, Dr. Maung Gyi and others in their 60s, 70s, and even 80s, still doing what they love, it is impressive and very inspiring.

They are role models for what it means to keep yourself in shape and to endure.

We all get injured and have aches and pains, but the ability to get up and get out there when your shoulder hurts, your hip aches, or your joints just don't feel good is what is motivating and makes us want to be that kind of person in the years to come.

A lot of times when I'm training my guys, it's that "old man" strength that helps motivate them. When they see me running bleachers and know I've had a hip replacement, a couple of knee surgeries and had this broke or that hurt, it makes them think, well, maybe I just need to suck it up and do it too.

24

CHAPTER THREE
DOS AND DON'TS

In the opening minute of the first round, you work to calm your jitters. You go over for the 1,000th time your list of dos and don'ts. Don't be overly aggressive during the initial adrenaline rush. Set the pace and control the ring. Watch out for the uppercut. Don't allow a takedown. Throw your best combinations and finish with a kick.

Tendons rupture, bones break, cartilage tears, joints hyperextend and everything strains and bruises. It's a martial arts reality that injury happens. And when it happens to you, your initial response is very important. Long-term effects on such issues as recovery time, seriousness of injury, complications of injury, and even the degree of recovery that is possible may hinge on your initial reaction of having just been injured. Therefore, the proper handling of the first steps after injury can set the tone for the entire process from injury to final recovery.

To help you properly take those first steps, here are some important "dos and don'ts."

DON'T IGNORE THE INJURY

Being tough has its place. After all, we are martial artists and "gutting it out" through the pain is part of our training. But everybody gets injured, and to pretend that you are beyond being hurt simply opens the door to further injury and complications.

Our team doctor, Dr. David Klein, says that 95 percent of minor sprains generally heal regardless of what we do to treat them, but the truth is that a minor injury left untreated can become a major issue. Damage can become more extensive, perhaps even permanent. Further injury can occur because of your weakened state or because compensating for an injured area puts excessive strain on another area of the body.

Remember that our holistic approach recognizes the interdependency of the whole with all parts, and so to treat or ignore an injury is to treat or ignore the whole body. When injury strikes, be aware, accept the reality of it and act accordingly.

From Your Corner:
Bill "Superfoot" Wallace

When I first began having problems with my hip, if I had understood exactly what was wrong with it and let it rest and let it heal, I might not have had the serious problems I had to go through. I might not have had to suffer so much pain, loss of athleticism and, ultimately, hip replacement surgery.

I hear guys say, "Oh, I'll just work through it. It's okay. It'll quit after a while."

No, it won't. It'll only get worse! Let it heal. Give it the rest it needs, the attention it needs, and give it the time it needs to properly heal.

DO TREAT THE INJURY IMMEDIATELY

When injury strikes, don't decide to go one more round, do one more set or wait until your class (or your day) is over before addressing it. Doing so can unnecessarily complicate the issue. If you suffer an injury, tend to it as soon as possible.

Some of the most commonly suffered injuries among martial artists are sprains and strains. These are pulls, tears, and over-extensions of connective tissue and muscle that can result in mild discomfort, or require surgery to repair. Here is the difference: A "sprain" is an injury to the ligament, the fibrous cords that connect bone to bone, whereas a "strain" is an injury to either a muscle or a tendon, the fibrous cords that connect bone to muscle. You "sprain" a ligament when you throw a kick, land badly and turn or twist your ankle. Or perhaps you fall, catch yourself with your arm and hyperextend your elbow. In both cases, you have a sprain to a ligament. Examples of suffering a "strain" might be a pulled groin or lower back muscle, a tear or rupture in a biceps tendon, or damage to the muscle and tendons in the hyperextended elbow mentioned above.

Sprain vs. Strain

- **SPRAIN: An injury to a ligament, the fibrous cords that connect bone to bone.**

- **STRAIN: An injury to a tendon, the fibrous cords that connect bone to muscle, or injury to a muscle.**

Again, if you sprain or strain yourself, or even if you don't know what the damage is, you need to do something. One of the common staples for early treatment of sprains and strains is known as R.I.C.E., which stands for **R**est, **I**ce, **C**ompression and **E**levation. R.I.C.E. is most effective during the first 24 to 48 hours after an injury and is the long standing go-to remedy used by EMTs and athletic trainers. R.I.C.E. is also something that you can do for yourself. Here is how you do it:

- **Rest:** Take the pressure off the injury immediately. You may be able to "walk off" some cramps, but if there is damage to the muscle, ligament or tendon tissue, additional movement and use of the injured body part may simply make things worse. So let the injured limb rest a day or two to see if it is going to heal okay. Then try to ease back into your normal routine. If it hasn't healed, you will know it.

- **Ice:** Cooling the affected area will help prevent excessive swelling and also help with the pain. If you watch professional basketball, notice what those million dollar players use on their injuries: ice. So treat yourself like a million dollars and ice. One of the best ice packs you can use is a plastic bag filled about three-fourths with ice. Pour enough water in it to make it softly conform to the contours of your injured body part. Put a towel over your skin (never ice directly on the skin—it could cause frostbite, the freezing of cells), and apply your pack for about 15 to 20 minutes. Let your skin rest for an hour, make sure that warmth and the sense of feeling has returned, and then you can ice again if you want.

- **Compression:** Oftentimes, a bandage or wrap will significantly benefit an injury. The pressure of the wrap can help reduce excessive swelling in tissues, and the rigidity of the wrap can immobilize and protect an injured area. Wrap the affected area completely with each turn of the wrap overlapping about half of the previous one. Be careful not to wrap too tightly as this can inhibit circulation. You want the wrap snug enough to immobilize the area, but not to the point of feeling tingly or turning blue. Use your wrap for as long as you are icing, but if you are not significantly better in a day or two, seek professional medical help.

- **Elevation:** If you can rest with an injury elevated higher than your heart, you can sometimes benefit from the pull of gravity as it helps pull excess fluids out of swollen tissues and prevent them from pooling.

Just as there are differences in severity, so are there differences in required treatment. The more mild the injury, the less treatment it will need and the more quickly it will respond. On the other end of the spectrum, a severe injury such as a ruptured tendon may require surgery.

There are three basic levels of severity for sprains and strains:

- **Class I:** Mild. No tearing of tendons or ligaments. Minimal swelling, you can still bear weight on it and move.
- **Class II:** Moderate. Partial tear of fibers. Moderate swelling and pain. Hurts to move and bear weight.
- **Class III:** Severe. Complete tear or rupture of fibers. Severe swelling and loss of function.

Whether sprained or strained, something is injured, probably hurts, and needs immediate attention. So here is the rule of thumb: If you feel like you may need to see a doctor, then it is probably a good idea to see one. It's better to just go and make certain. If you properly use the R.I.C.E. method and the problem hasn't cleared up in one or two days, then you need to seek medical attention.

From Your Corner: Dr. David Klein

The initial, moderate swelling and inflammation of an injury can actually bring some healthy benefits. As the body's first response to an injury or a breakdown, it can include beneficial actions such as causing platelets to aggregate for clotting purposes and fibroblasts to migrate to the area, start secreting collagen to bind things together and start the mending process. So one thing you do not want to do is to take drugs such as aspirin, ibuprofen and naproxen until several days after the injury because they can actually retard these needed healing processes.

DON'T SELF DIAGNOSE

Are you a qualified medical professional? Are you educated, trained and experienced enough to correctly diagnose injury? Do you have the right equipment and the appropriate initials after your name? Are you focused enough to objectively examine yourself and come to an unbiased and medically sound conclusion?

No?

Then don't do it.

You wouldn't let an unqualified person work on your car, prepare your tax return or even keep your dog. So in the instance of injury, don't go it alone. Don't decide for yourself the nature and extent of your injury. If simple measures such as R.I.C.E. don't alleviate the symptoms in a short time, see a professional.

From Your Corner:
Danny Dring

My shoulder was hurting a couple years of ago, but I continued to just work through it because I had the old blood-and-guts mentality. I thought I was taking care of it, applying balm, doing plenty of warm-ups, icing after workout, but it kept aching. It continued bothering me even when I was using ice and ibuprofen after training and doing a lot of physical therapy.

After several months, I finally decided to go see a doctor, who scheduled an MRI to further diagnose what was wrong. But the very next day while grappling, my bicep tendon ruptured and rolled down my arm under my skin. While I had felt the pain in my shoulder, the real issue was that my bicep tendon was fraying like a rope that had been partially cut.

Had I not been such a tough guy and just gone to seek out qualified medical advice earlier, I might have been able to negate some of the severity of the injury. I also may not have had to have the kind of surgery to reattach my bicep tendon back into the bone. Maybe it could have been mended, sewn and taken care of instead. Maybe I could have avoided a very comprehensive surgery and the long rehabilitation that followed.

DO IDENTIFY THE INJURY

As best you can, get an idea of the specific area of injury, its causes and extent. Here are a few sample questions to help you get those answers:

- What hurts? Is it your back? Then where exactly is the pain focused? Does your arm ache? Is it in the muscle or joint?
- What were you doing when the injury occurred?
- What makes it feel better?
- What makes it feel worse?

- Is there discoloration or swelling?
- Did something pop, break or get hyperextended?
- Is it chronic, meaning that it is an ongoing issue that doesn't seem to be getting better?
- Is it acute, meaning that it happened suddenly?
- Does it quickly subside so that you very soon feel better (such as a muscle spasm or "getting the breath knocked out of you")?
- In other words, just how much about your injury can you communicate?

One of the reasons this self-examination is important is that if professional medical attention is needed, you will be better able to describe your injury to your doctors. This will in turn enable them to better and more accurately treat your injury.

Your injured body is trying to tell you what is wrong. Listen to it so you can tell others.

DON'T USE PAIN AS A MEASUREMENT OF INJURY OR RECOVERY

Pain is a terrible measurement of injury and a completely unreliable method of diagnosis for several reasons.

First, pain is an extremely unique experience to an individual because everyone has his own threshold of pain tolerance. The martial arts are full of examples of building up tolerance to pain. For example, the martial artist that has practiced joint locks to the wrists and arms for years may be able, on injury, to accept the pain and continue to a far greater degree than the martial artist who has not been exposed to those kinds of disciplines. The developed ability to endure punches and kicks, being hit with a stick or other weapon, and even exposure to the elements can translate to greater pain tolerance upon and following an injury. But to the untrained, and even among trained individuals, there is a wide spectrum in terms of pain tolerance.

Also, if a person is currently taking medications for pain relief, the pain of an injury or impending injury may not register properly. Masked by the medication, the pain that should have acted as a warning sign can be overlooked.

Pain is also a unique experience for different parts of the human body. Simply put, what hurts in one place doesn't hurt in another. The arrangement of pain sensors in the body is far from consistent, and that makes the experience of pain inconsistent as well. For instance, in submission fighting, a shoulder lock is a safer technique for a fighter rather than a kneebar because it communicates more pain. The shoulder, having a lot more pain sensors in it than a knee can be screaming in pain under pressure that the knee would hardly notice, thus letting the fighter know he should tap out. Knees are full of cartilage and ligaments that simply don't have the same nervous structure as the muscles and tendons of a shoulder. When caught in a kneebar you may feel a lot of pressure but negligible pain, until it pops.

Another drawback of using pain to gauge injury is that pain in one area may originate in another. Think of the symptoms of a heart attack. Chances are you know that a heart attack may cause pain in the left arm. But is the left arm injured? Not at all, the pain originates in the heart and is transferred, or "referred," to the arm.

In the same way, many other injuries may cause a focus of pain in an area other than the place of injury. Kicks to the midsection, for example, may cause an injury to an internal organ such as the liver or gallbladder, but you may feel the pain in your shoulder. A bulging disc in the neck can cause pain, tingling and numbness in the arm, hand and fingers. The grappling injury to the bicep tendon mentioned in this chapter caused pain in the shoulder. An injury to the ligament in your hip joint may refer pain down your leg into your big toe. Lower back ligament damage can also cause pain in the legs, knees or anywhere else in the lower limbs.

Commom Martial Arts Injuries

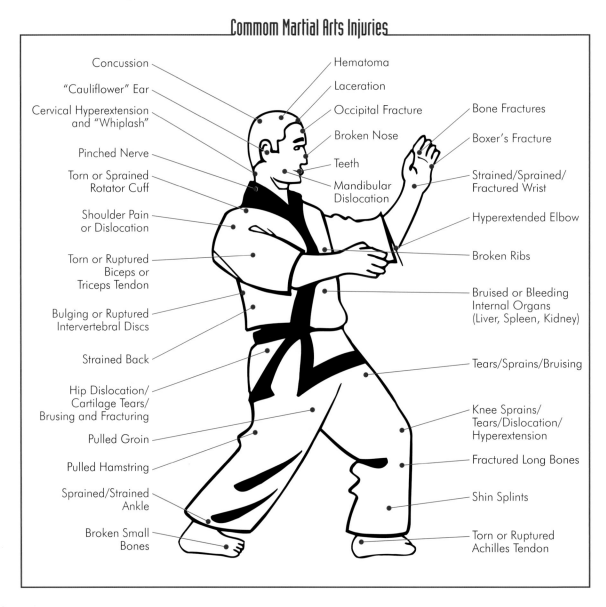

The point is that pain can often be only a symptom of the root cause. Therefore, the pain experienced cannot be the measurement of injury severity nor will treating the pain necessarily fix the problem. You can't fix the nerve by easing arm pain. You can't fix a ruptured bicep tendon by icing a shoulder.

Pain can't be used to measure recovery any more than for measuring injury, and for many of the same reasons. For example, what is wrong with the following "logic?"

- "It doesn't hurt anymore, so I don't need to complete my physical therapy regimen."
- "It hurts like crazy, so I'm not going to do my shoulder range of motion exercises anymore."
- "It doesn't hurt when I work out with light weights, so I must be ready for heavy lifting."
- "It hurts when I move it, so that must mean I'm working the soreness out."

As you can see, a person's interpretation of pain can lead to all sorts of wrong conclusions. Sometimes painful therapy is necessary. Other times pain is an indication of imminent injury or re-injury. So don't let your pain level dictate your activities; you need more reliable information than that.

DO SEEK PROFESSIONAL MEDICAL HELP

If your early efforts such as R.I.C.E. don't bring about a rapid improvement, then it is time to see a professional.

Don't just put it off.

Don't see what else you can try.

Don't do all those things mentioned in the "don'ts" of this section. Go get it checked out.

Perhaps you have a chronic injury and have been able to continue training for a while. However, instead of getting better, the pain is staying the same or getting worse. Perhaps you have adjusted your training routines and regimens to compensate for it and give it a "rest" while you train in other ways, but it still isn't well. See a doctor.

If you cannot in good conscience consider the injury to be "minor," then go get checked out by a qualified medical professional.

If one injury seems to be leading to other issues so that your overall level of health, wellness, and athleticism are declining, then it is time to seek medical advice.

If an injury weighs on your mind, adding to your mental stress, do all you can to cure it, and that definitely includes getting professional medical treatment.

If you would like to know all your options in terms of treatments, therapies, medications, etc., then go ask your medical professionals. Only they can educate you, interact with you and give you expert advice.

My bicep tendon ruptured in two and rolled down my arm at school one day. I knew without a doubt that I was injured, but I didn't know how severely. I just knew I would have to see a doctor.

Over a lifetime of being punched, kicked, and torqued, a person develops a fairly high tolerance for pain, so I was able to take a few minutes to immobilize my arm and arrange for someone to take my place at my school. Then Mr. Taylor drove me to the doctor while I made the necessary phone calls to family and colleagues.

There are people who never get such an injury repaired. They just continue their lives without full use of their bicep muscles. But as a martial artist, that was not an option for me. I wanted to keep doing what I love, and that means training and playing at my martial arts at full force. The only way I could continue was through competent and professional medical help.

DON'T GIVE UP!

An injury can be a very disheartening event, with repercussions that seem to permeate every aspect of a martial athlete's life. Take heart and determine to stay in the fight. In the grand scheme of life, the odds of you being able to make a significant, if not complete, recovery are actually pretty good.

CHAPTER FOUR
KNOW YOUR CORNER

In the ring, you hear the crowd cheer—some voices are for you and some are not. Above the din, you hear the voices from your corner. There is your coach, teammates, your fans and supporters. They are your team to give you encouragement, advice and the benefit of their distinct and objective perspective as they watch the fight. They will help you not only stay in the fight but get the "W." You know you wouldn't be here very long—or at all—if it weren't for the help and support of your corner.

The martial arts are individual sports, but just because you are the only one in the ring, it doesn't mean that there is not a team involved. On the contrary, you have many people in your corner. There is your coach or instructor, training partners, fans and supporters. They are all part of the team that is going to help you get the "W." You know you wouldn't be here very long—or at all—if it weren't for the help and support of your team.

Every fighter needs a team in his corner, and a fighter that is injured needs the best team he can put together. Your team may include doctors, therapists, coaches, writers, martial arts experts, masseuses, friends, family and others. If you try to go it alone without a rock-solid team to lend multidimensional support, you are setting yourself up for failure and defeat. If you can put together a team of qualified experts and committed supporters, you will multiply your chances of successful recovery.

Let's consider choosing a "cut man" for your corner to look at some principles to use in selecting a team of medical professionals to get you through a time of injury. We will address specifically the choice of a doctor and let this stand as a template for the selection of other professionals as well.

With that in mind, not all doctors are created equal, and even among the best of doctors, they are not all the best choice for you and your particular physical needs. So you need a way to sort through the many medical professionals out there. You need to pick the right doctor for you, one who will be the best fit for your team and do the best job in your corner.

This chapter covers eight questions to ask about a prospective doctor.

1. IS THE DOCTOR QUALIFIED?

Does he have the necessary initials after his name? Oddly enough, there are those who go by the title "doctor" who are not graduates of any recognized medical school.

The education and experience of a good doctor is invaluable to you in the healing process. You are going to put yourself into the hands of this person for some very serious issues, and you are going to follow his directions and advice to the letter. Check him out.

From Your Corner:
Danny Dring

I am not going to just turn my care over blindly to another person. I want to be able to ask questions, be informed, do my homework and intelligently seek second opinions. So here's what I recommend: Get a small digital recorder to take to your doctor appointments. When the doctor comes in, you may be traumatized, hurt, doped up or stressed out. He is going to blow in, talk a lot, and you won't know what he is saying. So tape him.

Tape him if it is allowable, get his advice, and refer back to the recording later. What you think you hear while you are upset and what you hear later on tape may be different.

Remember, too, that doctors don't always speak in layman's terms, and you may need to do some research later. Also, you may have family members who want to know what the doctor said. If you don't feel like repeating the information, give them your recorder.

SORTING THROUGH THE INITIALS: WHAT KIND OF DOCTOR?

A Medical Doctor (M.D.) may specialize in one of more than twenty recognized areas of expertise. A Doctor of Osteopathy (D.O.) is similar to an M.D. but with added emphasis on whole-body (holistic) treatment, the musculoskeletal system, and using their hands to diagnose and treat in a way similar to chiropractic and massage.

Here (in alphabetical order) are some of the specialties that are more commonly needed by an injured athlete:

- **Cardiology:** heart, blood vessels, and circulation

- **Emergency Medicine:** emergency-room care; preliminary care for a wide range of conditions, and identifies the correct specialist for further care

- **Endocrinology:** body chemistry, cellular functions and metabolic issues

- **Family Practice:** total care of the patient, and coordinating with specialists as needed; generally a primary care physician

- **General Surgery:** wide variety of surgery

- **Internal Medicine:** general medical treatment of adults; concerned with overall body health; may further specialize in areas such as gastroenterology (digestive system), infectious diseases and sports medicine

- **Neurology:** nervous system

- **Orthopedic Surgery:** musculoskeletal system; bones, joints, muscles, tendons, etc.; can prescribe medication and perform surgery

- **Otolaryngology:** ear, nose and throat; can include plastic surgery

There are also dozens if not hundreds of subspecialities, many nationally recognized organizations that enable a doctor or specialist to become "board certified," and there is an endless list of particular certifications that they can achieve and of training courses they can complete.

2. IS THE DOCTOR SPECIALIZED?

Some doctors specialize in heart and lung issues, some in geriatrics and some in pediatrics. The list of specializations in the medical field is almost endless, so it makes good sense to find a doctor that specializes in your type of medical needs. Is he a sports medicine doctor? Does he treat athletes? If not, he may be a good doctor but not a good match for your team. For a toothache, you would find a dentist. As a martial artist, find someone who understands your type of injury.

Beyond that, there are also many schools of thought concerning health and wellness. There is a wide range of philosophies, attitudes and practices among doctors, and common sense tells you that there are going to be some very good physicians, some very bad ones and many in the middle. Find a specialist that you can be comfortable with.

Some of the more prominent organizations (in alphabetical order) include:

- **American College of Sports Medicine (ACSM)**
- **American Medical Society for Sports Medicine (AMSSM)**
- **American Orthopaedic Society for Sports Medicine (AOSSM)**
- **American Osteopathic Academy of Sports Medicine (AOASM)**

We should note that "sports medicine" is not an official medical specialty. Any doctor can claim to practice it. If they say they specialize in sports medicine, it may mean they have achieved a set of certifications and training emphases for sports-related medical issues.

So to help simplify matters, here are a few pieces of information you want to find out about a prospective doctor:

- What sports medicine organization is s/he a member of?
- How long has s/he been treating athletes?
- What percentage of their clients are athletes? (30 or 40 percent is a good number)
- Is s/he the team physician for anyone?
- What is his/her specialty?

Another way to possibly simplify the matter is to ask your primary care physician if any medical specialist is needed and if he can recommend an appropriate specialist for you to consider. He probably knows his local medical community well and often refers patients to specialists. Be sure to speak to him in a respectful, professional manner that is appreciative of any help he can offer you. Of course, he should answer you in the same tone. After all, your primary care physician is "in your corner."

The problem with putting together a team of physicians is that they are very individualistic and unique. Each has his or her own viewpoint, philosophies and tendencies so that you may receive a wide range of advice on any given subject.

Add to that the parameters involved with searching for specific types of physicians, and you can see it can be even more difficult.

Remember, your condition dictates who you are trying to see, why you want to see them and when. If you are trying to find a good orthopedic surgeon, for example, it may be very difficult. If you are looking for a good cardiologist, you may have to go to a different town. You want a good endocrinologist? You may have to go to a different state.

To further complicate things, remember that a specialist specializes for reasons. For example, an orthopedic surgeon may be more apt to recommend surgery since that is his specialty. Add to all this your desire for a physician who knows and understands the nature of a martial arts injury, and you can see how difficult it is to find one person who can do everything you need done.

Instead, when possible you want to find several different individuals who can give you different pieces of advice. Then it will be up to you to choose your course of action and your team of medical professionals.

3. IS THE DOCTOR ATHLETIC?

If your doctor is an athlete, you may feel better about his ability to treat you because he probably shares the athlete's psyche—you two are more in tune. If, on the other hand, he is a smoker, overweight or looks sickly, then his personal practices may not give you much confidence in his medical practices. If he doesn't share your values, or understand why an athletic level of health and wellness is of vital importance to you, then you have to wonder if he is a good fit for your team. If his advice is to go home, take some pills and do nothing, it should probably make you wonder if he really knows what is best for you.

So what kind of doctor do you want? You want a doctor who knows how important it is for you to get back to your chosen athletic endeavors as quickly and effectively as possible. You want him to understand that you can suck up some pain and that you are already highly motivated to heal as quickly as possible. You want him to understand that your definition of who you are is to a great extent shaped and formed by your ability to go play martial arts.

4. IS THE DOCTOR EMPATHETIC?

Because of your martial arts mind-set, you want your doctor to not only be athletic but also empathetic to your situation. He needs to understand that you are not just another athlete with an injury, but that your injury represents a major concern in many areas of your life. After all, a professional martial artist is in obvious danger of a loss of income and possibly even a career.

Even an amateur martial artist finds that injury takes a toll on his life. Can you drive to work with a cast on your foot? Can you type your reports with a bandaged hand or shoulder? Can you really afford to take six weeks off work to rest at home, ice every hour and keep your injured area elevated? In short, does the doctor know what down time will cost you?

You think: I need to get back as quickly and safely as I can. Can I train or work around my injury? When can I put stress on it? An empathetic doctor will understand these concerns.

I walked into an orthopedic surgeon's office and realized I was the youngest person there by twenty or thirty years. I wondered if this guy was going to be able to help me, understand me and identify with me as an athlete.

I went to another one, and half the people in the waiting room were obviously active athletes. I felt a little more comfortable and thought maybe the doctor sees more people like me. I'm not saying the other guy wasn't a good doctor, but I'm hedging my bets. I wanted someone who is used to getting athletes back up and running.

5. IS THE DOCTOR INTERACTIVE?

Every team player knows that communication is key. You need a doctor who will communicate with you.

Will he take time with you? Will he listen to your concerns and answer your questions? If you are going to do your part in optimizing your healing, then you need to understand the doctor's explanations and instructions.

Many doctors are busy and overworked. You can feel rushed. You may not feel clearly understood and you may not understand the medical jargon they use. They aren't mind readers. They don't know your particular concerns and are not aware of your situation and individual needs. If they aren't willing to deal around your needs, maybe they are not right for you. However, if they will listen and interact with you, they will better be able to help you in your healing process. Ask the right questions respectfully as a professional, and they should respond respectfully as a professional.

6. IS THE DOCTOR COMPREHENSIVE?

There was a time when an injury was handled with a cast, sling, surgery, pain pills, bed rest and that's about it.

Today there is a wide range of protocols in use for healing injuries, and you want your doctor to offer them. Find out if he believes in the benefits of different types of treatment, modalities and the use of medical technologies. You also need to know if he will get you an MRI or X-ray if you need one and if there are additional directions and therapies that can optimize your healing.

Some doctors' diagnosis and treatment are closely dictated by what is allowed by the insurance industry. You need to know if he is bound to follow their designated protocols whether they are right for you or not, or if he is going to try as many good options as needed to help you stay in the fight.

From Your Corner:
Johnny D. Taylor

My chiropractor told me that one of the best preventions, if not cures, for not only my chronic back problems but also for the mitigation of the onset of arthritis in my spine is a good stretching regimen. She gave me plenty of stretches to perform, showed me X-rays of where the spine was starting to develop some spurs and arthritis, and explained how flexibility exercises and weight bearing exercises would help keep it at bay. I appreciated the fact that she was very comprehensive.

7. IS THE DOCTOR AVAILABLE?

In many areas, doctors are so busy that it is difficult to see them, and getting an appointment in a timely manner may be even harder. When you move beyond the need for a primary care physician and search for a specialist, the hunt for the right person can be even more difficult.

There are some questions you need answered concerning the medical professional before you even talk to them about your injury. They are:

- Is s/he taking new patients?
- Is s/he covered by your insurance?
- If s/he is a specialist, does s/he (or your insurance) require a referral from your primary care physician?
- Is s/he affordable?
- Will you be allowed to pay out your bill in installments if necessary? In the arena of your own personal health, healing and wellness, only you are qualified to determine how much you can spend on your care, but it should go without saying that you want the best care available.

Be warned that if you don't take care of this business end of finding the right doctor, you may find yourself very much at odds with your insurance company, then your doctor's office. Clearing up the issues of availability, insurance coverage and required prerequisites such as referrals can save you a lot of headaches during and after your treatment. While you are being treated for injury, the last thing you need is a medical business problem.

These questions and others can usually be answered by the person who answers the phone at the doctor's office. Just list out the questions you need answered, give them a call and collect your information.

8. IS THE DOCTOR RECOMMENDED?

How do you get answers to all these questions? How do you sort through all the medical professionals out there? One way is to find recommendations. You aren't the first patient the doctors have had. They all have a reputation; you just need to research it.

Here are a few places to look and see who comes highly recommended:

- **Locally:** Ask local trainers, coaches and other athletes whom they use and would recommend. Call the high schools, colleges and universities and ask the athletic department for recommendations. Ask them who the team doctor is for the school. Ask people for the three best doctors for shoulder, hip or whatever your concern. A few names will rise to the top.
- **Professionally:** Research your prospective doctor on the Internet. Is the practice listed? Does the doctor have articles in medical journals and magazines? Have they won any awards? Have they been involved in malpractice lawsuits? The Internet is a great source of information that can often give you a good feel for the doctor's particular style and strengths.

These are issues to settle with not only the selection of a medical doctor, but with other medical professionals as well. There is no substitute for having a great medical team in your corner. You are going to put yourself in their hands, listen carefully to everything they tell you and follow their advice and orders to the letter. They are going to optimize your healing, and your confidence in their ability and expertise will lend a deeper sense of peace and positivity in your mind while you recover.

CHAPTER FIVE
REDEFINE YOUR GOALS

*In the ring, your opponent is prodding, testing your defenses and sizing you up.
He is trying to figure you out. But you have already done your homework;
you have studied your opponent. You already know his strengths, weaknesses,
style, favorite techniques, his record and level of experience.
After all, "know thy enemy" has been good advice for centuries, and you know
exactly who you are up against and what to do with the knowledge.*

Your goal was to compete in a tournament, advance in rank or beat your personal best. But injury has left you sitting on the sideline, watching your goals and plans fall apart in your hands. What are you supposed to do now? Where do you go from here? What did the doctor mean by those medical terms he used to explain your injury?

These are valid (and commonly asked) questions to which you need answers. It is the very idea of goals that you need to focus on at this time.

It may be that your doctor has told you to go home and do basically nothing, that rest and inactivity are what you need. Doing nothing, however, is difficult for a martial athlete, and it is a sorry excuse for a goal. So your downtime may be the perfect time to take stock of your situation, redirect yourself and redefine your goals.

Chances are you are a goal-oriented person, understanding the importance of setting and reaching goals not just as a method of martial arts advancement but as a lifestyle. Just because injury has struck doesn't mean that goal setting is no longer for you. It means that your goals must be redefined.

The truth is that you redefine your goals all the time whether you are aware of it or not. In a sparring match, you set a goal of round-kicking your opponent in the ribs. But he steps in, spins and plants a back kick heel deep into your stomach. You immediately redefine your goal. Old goal: Round-kick. New goal: Circle to safety and breathe.

Or perhaps your goal of landing your jab causes your opponent to cover his field of vision and leave his legs open. Old goal: Jab. New goal: Fake the jab and go for a takedown.

The same thing should happen with injury. The old goals of competition and advancement may have to be put on the back burner for a while, but they are to be replaced with new goals that focus you on returning to optimal health. Perhaps your new goals should include things such as injury research, daily stretching, physical therapy sessions, proper diet and hydration, range of motion exercises … . The list can go on and on and depends on your specific situation.

You must harness your goal-achieving abilities and apply them to the task at hand. You are still in the fight, but the fight has changed. You have a new list of opponents, and so you must understand them, put together a plan that will bring you victory over them, and set goals that will take you from where you are to where you want to be. That is what is meant by redefining your goals.

STEP 1: UNDERSTAND YOUR OPPONENT

The first step to redefining your goals is to educate yourself about your injury. Like any other fight, ignorance of this opponent places you at a distinct disadvantage. Not knowing what to expect or not understanding the nature and far-reaching effects of an injury can hinder your recovery and make the entire process more of an ordeal than is necessary. Remember the old warrior adage: "To be forewarned is to be forearmed."

So what should you study?

Begin by educating yourself on the specifics of your injury. After all, if you don't know what's wrong, how can you fix it? So find out how extensive your injury is, how common it is, what can be done about it, and what it is going to take to get you back to health and wellness.

To learn the specifics, you'll need to study the nature of your particular injury, too. You need to educate yourself on your own anatomy and get a good understanding of which muscles, bones, tendons, tissues and physical systems are affected. What about the surrounding tissues? What about the supporting systems of the injured area? Is it a sprain, strain, tear, rupture, bruise or break? Is it cartilage or bone, infection or syndrome, chronic or acute? What exactly has happened to you?

In addition to understanding the problem, you must also understand the solutions. What are the common protocols for the treatment of your type of injury? What is the standard, and what are the latest treatment options for optimized healing? Remember that part of your process is communicating and working with your "corner," and you need to be able to interact effectively with your doctor and other medical professionals. Communication means you need to understand the medical terminology they will be using, be able to ask intelligent and educated questions, and understand their answers.

While you're injured and recovering, you should definitely begin prepping for your rehabilitation. Determine what physical systems need to be addressed, not just the specific injury. For instance, if you have a back muscle injury, you need to learn what to do for not only the injured muscle itself, but also what you can do to stabilize the rest of your core such as your abs and obliques.

Also find out what to expect not only in terms of rehabilitation, but how long it will probably take you to fully recover. Or, you should learn if full recovery is even possible. Having a timeline to follow to let you know what to expect and when to expect it, as well

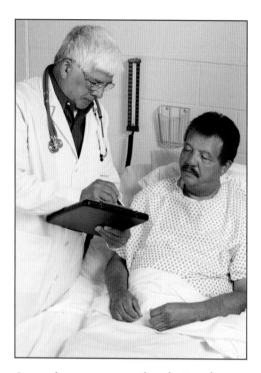

Once you have surgery, you go through a time when your medical professionals don't want you to do anything. It could be three weeks, six weeks or longer. So you map out your strategy during your downtime, educating yourself about the injury, surgery and protocols for treatment, therapy and rehabilitation, for instance. You make sure you are taking your supplements, icing and doing anything else you can be doing. You approach the whole thing like a workout.

as a framework on which to set goals for yourself, can prove to be invaluable. When will you be able to put weight on your injured body part? When will you be able to train with any impact or "resume normal activity?" When there is no more pain, and you are anxious to get back to training, what are the risks of re-injury?

Furthermore, you need to understand the long-term effects of your injury. What will life be like after your treatment, rehabilitation and comeback? What can you expect to be able to do or not do when it is all over? You are not asking these questions to set limits on yourself. Instead, you are asking these questions to prepare yourself for what you will face at the end of the process.

So where do you find all this information that you will need?

Ask your medical professionals. You want your own team of well-trained professionals to be your chief and "official" source for understanding your injury and your treatment. Not only are they in your "corner" but also their knowledge and experience are invaluable. There may be no rule of thumb for treating your particular injury, which means that you and your team may have to put together a customized protocol of treatments. They will also be able to explain how things work and why you must follow the details of your treatment to completion. They may even have materials and resources available for you to study to further your education of the injury and treatment. Ask them for brochures, Web site addresses and videos. Ask them also to take the time to explain in detail what you need to know about your injury. Your doctors' understanding of your injury and treatment can help prevent complications and associated injury and re-injury. Incisions can reopen and medications can have side effects, for example. These are just a few of the issues your medical professionals can help you understand.

You should also search the Internet. Chances are there is a ton of information about your injury and methods of treatment available. There are medical sites, sites devoted to specific injury, discussion groups and miracle cures for sale, to name just a few. You can research the anatomy of the injured area to get a better understanding of exactly what has happened to you, and you can also find out what treatments are standard and what is cutting edge. Of course, you should discuss your Internet research with your team. Remember that your return to health should be a group effort. Don't make decisions alone.

Also ask trainers, coaches and other athletes that have already gone through what you are facing. They may have personal experience and an understanding of your type of injury and recovery. Perhaps they can even recommend other contacts and resources to help you out.

Remember that, ultimately, you are responsible for your health and healing. So put yourself in good medical hands, but don't expect them to know and do everything for you. Educate yourself further and help the healing process along within the parameters of sound medical advice.

From Your Corner:
Danny Dring

After hip surgery, I was definitely stressing to get started exercising again. So I asked my doc about it.

"Yeah, yeah," he said. "We'll find you something to do. But stay off the hip." What he really wanted me to do was things like gentle range of motion exercises, and no weight bearing exercises. Sometimes you have to probe and ask questions.

Finally, when the stitches were out, I could get in the pool and do gentle range-of-motion exercises in the water. I could get some exercise for my upper body and do some non-weight bearing workouts without putting my body at risk for further injury or re-injury. I found something I could do that fit in the parameter of staying off my hip.

It was a good day when I could resume some physical activity.

From Your Corner:
Renegade Coach
John Davies

You have to understand your injury and know where the weakness really started. For instance, I can look back now at the injuries I had and see where they really originated. My severely ruptured hamstring may have actually started two years earlier. It could have been due to poor training techniques and protocols that my coach didn't recognize as well as flexibility issues, the way I was striking with my feet, and/or insufficient strength in my basic trunk.

If my coach had understood this at the time, he could have pulled me aside, done an assessment and corrected these issues before they culminated in significant injury.

STEP 2: PUT TOGETHER YOUR PLAN

As you educate yourself concerning your injury, you can begin to formulate your plan of attack. A plan is a roadmap to show how you are going to get from where you are to where you want to be. In your case, "where you are" is a state of injury and "where you want to be" is a state of optimal health and wellness.

A good roadmap explains things like modes of transportation, which roads will be taken, how long the trip is in both distance and time and the important sites along the way. In the same way, a good plan for injury recovery will include things like methods of

Here are some of the benefits of putting together a plan when dealing with injury:

- **Involvement:** Being involved in the healing process helps give a sense that you are more than a victim, more than just waiting to heal, but that you are carrying the fight to the enemy.

- **Mission:** You gain a sense of mission and purpose when you have set goals in your quest for health and healing.

- **Control:** Everything that you can do puts a bit of control back in your hands. When you feel like you are simply at the mercy of your injury, any way to regain a sense of control over your life is welcome.

- **Fights Boredom:** Being an active martial athlete and suddenly being told to do nothing for any length of time results in frustration and boredom. Having goals gives you plenty to do and helps optimize recovery time.

- **Goal-Setting Habit:** You know the importance of setting concrete goals for yourself, and though your earlier goals may be deferred, a new set of goals helps you keep the achievement mind-set.

- **Victories:** Reaching well-defined goals and achieving measurable progress means victories for you, both great and small, and that is just as true for your recovery goals as it is for your martial arts career goals.

therapy, medical protocols and exercises that will be used to promote healing. There will also be a list of your "team members," such as doctors and therapists, an idea of the time and effort involved, and most importantly a clear description of the "destination" of your maximized healing and wellness. After all, if you don't know where you are going, you won't know how to get there.

What might your "roadmap" look like? In terms of your own injury, recovery, health and wellness, you need to know what a comprehensive plan of attack would look like. Make a list of the details it would include such as resources needed and a recovery timeline.

Remember that one of the purposes of this book is to help you with just such an endeavor. There are work pages called Fightsheets for each chapter at the end of this book. As you complete each one, you will build a customized plan of attack to optimize your own health and healing.

From Your Corner:
Mark Graden, Former NAPMA Director of Curriculum

During recovery after surgery on my arm, it was tough just being sedentary. I had stitches and a full cast on, so I really couldn't do much of anything for exercise. If I started to sweat it would quickly turn rancid, and possibly set up infection, so I was looking at about six weeks with no activity at all. That seemed like a long time and made me anxious about the whole thing. It just drove me stir crazy, even to the point of being unable to sleep.

I knew I had a good plan though, and I had heard good things about the repairs returning me to 100 percent if I would do the right things. I made sure that I did them according to plan.

When I got aggravated about my condition, I would remind myself that it was really just a little while that I would have to be completely inactive, and then I would be able to train again. I knew that I was going to get back in there, it wasn't going to hold me back and it was absolutely a temporary setback. So, as with all the other injuries that I've had, I worked to have the best plan I could, to stay with it and to turn it into something positive.

STEP 3: SET (REDEFINED) GOALS

A goal is an achievement that is specific and measurable. Think of a basketball game, for example. The ball goes through the hoop or it doesn't; either you score or you don't; either you make a goal or you don't. The goal is specific (ball through the hoop) and measurable (two points).

Your goals in this process must meet the same criteria; they must be specific and measurable. General goals such as "getting better" or "doing push-ups" may fit nicely in the plan, but they aren't specific. Exactly how and when will you "get better," and how will you measure it? Exactly when, how often and how many push-ups will you do? When you write that down, you have a goal, which is specific and measurable. Either you do your push-ups or you don't. Either you increase the weight load from 10 pounds to 15 pounds over the next two weeks or you don't.

Now you can clearly measure your progress, make necessary adjustments along the way and turn a long and difficult journey into small, manageable sections. Here is a simple example to help you make sense of the process:

From Your Corner:
Johnny D. Taylor

I developed what turned out to be a bulging disc in my neck that caused pain and some weakness down my shoulder and arm and numbness in my hand and thumb. I spent some time ignoring it, giving it sporadic and ineffective treatments such as popping ibuprofen and wishing it would go away.

It didn't.

So I had to lay aside my old plans and goals, which included improved athleticism through lifting weights and running. It was now time for new goals to be defined. Here's what I did:

- **Plan:** First, I made a new plan. It included seeking professional help, conducting personal research on bulging neck discs and doing whatever else I thought would help me get better. Through the process I found that the best methods for me included applying ice instead of heat on my neck, sleeping with a rolled-up towel under my neck, and perhaps trying some visualization exercises for healing. (For more on visualization, see Chapter 10.)

Next, I needed to turn the elements of my plan into genuine goals. By examining my plan, I was able to determine what specific and measurable actions I needed to take that would result in accomplishing my plan. They included the following goals:

- **Goal:** I will call my chiropractor for the earliest appointment available.
- **Goal:** I will research my injury and symptoms on Tuesday evening and find out as much as possible about what the problem is and any recommended treatments.

After I had achieved these goals, I was able to set more:

- **Goal:** For 30 minutes each afternoon and at bedtime, I will ice my neck and rest it on a rolled-up towel.
- **Goal:** I will make regular visits to the chiropractor twice a week.
- **Goal:** Twice a week I will go to the gym and work my lower body because it is uninjured. If I do any upper-body exercises, I will only do those that do not aggravate my condition.
- **Goal:** I will add visualization exercises to my routine twice daily: afternoon and bedtime.

After a few weeks of that, it was time to take stock again and redefine my goals:

- **Goal:** The chiropractic adjustments haven't helped, but the visualization, icing and towel have. Today I will cancel my chiropractic appointments and start doing my visualization exercises three times a day. I will continue icing and using the towel under my neck.

A couple of months later, all my symptoms were gone except for a little residual numbness in the tip of my thumb. So did this mean I could jump back to my old routine? No! It was time to redefine my goals again:

- **Goal:** Next Monday, I will resume upper-body weightlifting using low weights and high repetitions and see how it goes. If I have no worsening of symptoms, I'll go back to my previous workout routines.
- **Goal:** If I experience an occasional flare up of symptoms, I will ice accordingly.
- **Goal:** I will make visualization and using the rolled-up towel under my neck permanent parts of my lifestyle.

As you can see, my recovery took quite a while but was almost 100 percent complete. Today I'm back to my old plans and goals, and the disc is not much of a consideration. For those rare times when I suffer a flare up of symptoms, I know just what to do about it.

Notice how the plans included general elements such as learning about the injury and deciding which medical professional to see, while the goals included specifics such as a Tuesday evening of Internet research and 30 minutes of ice. The idea is to put together a good plan and then set specific goals that will result in the completion of that plan.

Remember also that resetting and redefining your goals will be an ongoing process throughout the course of your recovery. There will not only be long-term goals such as making a full comeback and reestablishing your pre-injury goals, but there will also be many medium and short-term goals to get you from one leg of the journey to the next. It is therefore vital for you to consistently take these three steps:

- Educate yourself on all facets of your injury and recovery.
- Put together a good plan.
- Set and achieve goals.

Don't let your injury or situation in life convince you that you are already defeated. You are not finished, and you are not quitting. You may be down, but you are not out. You may have had a setback, but that sets the stage for a comeback. Be certain of this truth: You are still in the fight! So do your homework, hammer out a good plan using the Fightsheets and information in this book, and go to work.

CHAPTER SIX
TRAIN AROUND AN INJURY

You're feeling good. The fight is going your way.
All your hard training is paying off as your technique melds with your athleticism
and you score point after point. You have learned to build both defensive posture
and offensive counters into your techniques. Your arsenal is well supplied
so that if one technique doesn't work, another one will.

When injury strikes and medical care is necessary, it can often seem as though your athletic life has come to a complete halt. During this time of healing and recovery you may be under a doctor's close care, forced into inactivity, or slowly working your way through physical therapy. You can feel sidelined, left behind and at a loss as to what to do with yourself.

It is true that you are injured, that you have body parts that work weakly or not at all, and that your typical workout routines are out of reach while you are recovering. But it is equally true that even during this time of healing you are still a martial athlete, and you need to train to whatever degree possible. You obviously can't train the injured areas of your body, but you can probably train other areas. It may be completely possible to get a good workout without risk of further injury to your recovering or injured areas.

This idea of training around an injury can help keep you active and keep your body as strong as possible while healing takes place. In short, it simply means that while one part is injured, you can train something else. For example, if your knee or leg is out of commission, then train your upper body if possible. If your shoulder is hurt, then train your lower body. If your right arm is tender, perhaps you can at least work on your left jab. In this chapter, we will look at how to do just that.

TWO ASPECTS OF YOUR BODY: INJURED AND UNINJURED

First, you have to settle in your mind that there is more to your body than just injury. You are not one giant injury. There are probably plenty of body parts that still work, and you have to think of your body parts in terms of these two aspects: injured and uninjured. While the injured parts may have to be kept inactive, waiting until they are strong enough to resume activity, the uninjured parts may not have to wait at all. Also, varying degrees of injury dictate varying degrees of inactivity. For example, a strained tendon may not slow you down nearly as much as a ruptured tendon, and an arm in a sling may be able to handle more overall body activity than an arm in a cast.

Not all injuries require complete bed rest. Quite often, doctor's orders call for resting the affected area, so it may be that you are capable of getting in a good deal of exercise even while you are healing and recovering from an injury. If you haven't already done so, check with your medical professionals to determine just how much activity you are able to handle in your current situation and don't completely stop working out unless you have to.

So what are your uninjured, capable parts? If your injury is to your upper body, your lower body may be capable of working out, or vice versa. If your left arm is injured, your right arm may still be available. If your lower back is a problem, determine if your chest, arms and legs can still be exercised.

Once you know *what* you can work, you are ready to determine *how* you can work them. Remember that an injury is by nature a limitation, and you have a list of things that you are unable to do while you heal. Some are obvious, like no running on a broken leg. Some are due to doctor's orders, like no jarring or contact training. Here, your focus is not on what you cannot do but on what you *can* do, and that may include a lot.

In terms of the six dimensions of athletic health, the dimensions of strength, cardio and flexibility are the ones you will focus your workout on.

In terms of strength training, if your upper body is injured there are tons of lower body exercises such as squats and lunges you

When you go back to the gym, remember that you may still have technical knowledge and skill sets that your body can no longer perform. Be careful to work in accordance with what your recovering body can handle instead of trying to see what all you can still do.

may be able to perform. Many gyms have a row of weight machines that isolate lower body muscles and may allow you to get the entire workout you want. The same is true if you have a lower body injury, but a healthy upper body. Weight machines, free weights, dumbbells, and other equipment can be used to work the healthy parts while not engaging the injured or recovering parts. Just remember the importance of safety during this time when you are more vulnerable to additional injury. Be sure to use a spotter when you lift weights, for example.

For the dimensions of cardio and flexibility, you may also have many options. If you aren't cleared for the jarring of impact training such as kicking or punching, go with resistance training using light weights and high reps. If you can't pound the pavement or run bleachers, try a stationary bike, stair step machine, rowing machine, or an agility ladder. If you can get into a swimming pool then perhaps you can get a good cardio workout and improve your flexibility, even if you can only engage part of your body.

Be sure to talk to your medical professionals about any exercises you intend to do. There may be medical considerations of which you are unaware, and there may be a waiting period for certain types of exercises. Stitches may need to be protected from stretching, for example. Sweating while you are in a cast can not only cause a bad stink, but may breed bacteria that can lead to infection. Certain medications may preclude getting your heart rate up. You won't know until you ask.

If you can creatively train around your injury, you will minimize the loss of athleticism from injury, maintain a sense of overall fitness, maintain a certain martial skill level, get some endorphins and keep a positive outlook on life as you fight your way back to optimal health. You may even come out of this recovery time with a valuable set of new and improved skills that you would have never developed unless you had been injured. So build a good list of all your options and get started doing what you can, and remember that as your healing progresses you will be able to add more exercises to your workout routines.

From Your Corner: Danny Dring

When I was on crutches, I would sit on a box on the mats and do wrist locks and throws. Some creative cross-training helps keep you going.

From Your Corner: Johnny D. Taylor

As odd as it seems, an electric treadmill may be just the thing when you begin your recovery. You can set it for a very slow walk and hold onto the handrails, and this will begin to get you gently moving your entire body. You can do your warm-up on it without the jarring or jogging of calisthenics. You can do low impact cardio on it if you set it at a brisk walk on a high incline.

Another benefit of a long, slow walk on a treadmill is that it is boring. You are free to direct your full attention to other productive things such as instructional videos and mental exercises. You can do your visualization and self-coaching exercises (explained later in this book), and you can do the surprisingly hard work of focused thinking. In fact, slow treadmill work can gently increase your metabolism, heart rate and blood flow to the brain, resulting in heightened mental alertness. I've used it to solve many problems, settle many internal issues and keep my life's priorities in order, all while logging extra miles and hours of exercise.

In training, there are many different ways to perform a movement and many different exercises to accomplish your goal. You may have to change the way you do things and get innovative and creative, but that is what you do. You find a way to get top-quality training even though you are injured, and there isn't an exercise out there that doesn't have an alternative possibility.

For example, you may have to change the way you hold a bar so you can still do squats. Or, you may have to reduce an exercise to some very simple movements, but you never stop working.

TRAIN YOUR SKILLS

Another way to train around your injury is to practice your skills and technique. The very things that set the martial arts apart from other athletic endeavors are the skills and techniques we use. Strikes, kicks, takedowns, submissions, position, forms, speed and control: these are valuable and hard-won abilities for the martial artists, and they need to be maintained to whatever degree is possible, even during times of injury. As a martial athlete, you know that you would never sacrifice technical expertise for physical conditioning anyway, and so maintaining skill levels are very important.

In your current situation, how much can you focus on skill development? If you can still do your forms, then do them, even if you can't include your whole body. If you have to, do the footwork portion only, or do the upper body motions and imagine your lower body doing the rest. Can you do four-count kicks? Then do them as best you can. Practice your footwork and your shadowboxing. If your right arm is out of commission, work on your left jab and hook. Work your kicks and the grappling skills that focus on legwork.

Think back over the many lessons you have had and the many skills you have been exposed to. Chances are that there is a significant list of skill-specific activities and exercises that you can do to some degree without risk of further injury. Find them and do them.

Think also about all the other martial arts styles and disciplines that there are. From Brazilian *jiu-jitsu* to kickboxing, from *tai chi* to *Krav Maga*, from self-defense to swords, the world of martial arts contains a multitude of skills, techniques and styles. How many of them can you work on while you are recovering? You can practice self-defense moves and wrist locks while sitting in a chair or on the floor. You can work on traditional *taekwondo* stances, even with your arm in a cast. Many disciplines make use of a *gi*, therefore having a proper and powerful grip is a good skill to learn and develop.

What would you like to learn? Find out, see if you can do it safely, then do it.

What other sports and physical activities interest you? If you give it some thought and study, you can probably come up with even more exercises you can do as you train around your injury. There is wheelchair basketball and table tennis to keep your hand-eye coordination sharp. If you can't use your arms, perhaps you can play soccer, or at least use soccer exercises for lower body agility and balance. Not long ago, playing hacky sack was popular. It isn't very martial, but it's something to do and builds balance, timing and coordination. Even video games can get you moving. The one that rhymes with "T" has a wide variety of games, sports and skill levels.

From Your Corner: Mark Graden, Former NAPMA Director of Curriculum

While I was recovering from my ruptured bicep tendon, I couldn't spar with my students. Instead, I did more coaching from the side, and that benefited them.

Another example is that three months before a world title fight in Europe, I broke my toe and couldn't kick. So, I worked a lot on my defense and my hands. During that time I had a major acceleration in those areas. Was it a bad thing that I broke my toe? Of course it was, but my defense ended up being better.

What is really important is the end result, training in all kinds of ways and always getting better.

PERMANENT INJURY

It is a fact that not all injury can be recovered from and not all wounds heal. In the case of permanent injury and damage to the body, the idea of training around that injury becomes even more important because you are not just filling in a gap of time until your injured parts are whole again; you may very well be reinventing yourself as a martial artist.

Just remember that if you can move, you can be an athlete. While some injuries are easier to train around than others, odds are you can still find a martial arts discipline and skill set that meets your needs and suits your situation. We will more fully address these issues later on in this book, but for now, here is some inspiration from Bill Wallace:

As life changes, so will your potential. Your desire to maximize that potential should never change. Always challenge yourself.

A long time ago, I was a judo practitioner. While I was training for the California state championships in 1966, I tore the medial ligament in my right knee, which in turn tore some of the meniscus on the medial side. I ended up in a cast from the crotch to my right ankle.

I figured my judo career was over. But when I got out of the cast, I went by a karate school to check out some lessons and see what was possible. The instructor asked me what was wrong with me, and I told him my story.

"Okay," he said. "Join the class."

"But I have a bad knee," I said.

"Only kick with your left leg," he said. "When we kick with the left leg, you kick with your left leg, too, and when we kick with the right leg, you just keep kicking with your left one. Just stay with your left side forward, even when the rest of the class switches to right side forward."

Even though the injury was permanent, he taught me to train around it. This led to me becoming a national point-fighting champion, then a kickboxing champion wherein I was able to retire undefeated.

CHAPTER SEVEN
POSTHAB

In the ring, you constantly remind yourself to keep a strong defense up. This guy is no joke, and when he lands one, you feel it. You know that if his first punch hurts, his second one will be worse. So you keep your hands up, move your head, slip his punches, back peddle and tuck your chin. It is much more fun to be hit at and missed. Now your opponent has taken his best shot and expended a great deal of energy. But your defenses held; you are still standing. Now it's your turn.

Congratulations, you are officially healed! You have finished your course of medication, went to all your follow-up visits and completed all the therapy sessions that the doctor has prescribed (and that your insurance company will pay for). You finally get to hear those wonderful words from your doctor: "You are free to resume normal activity."

As a martial artist, however, you know that "normal activity" is not a good description of what you do. In fact, your training is probably "extreme" compared to what many other people do. In addition, your injury, though physically healed, has left the affected areas of your body in a weakened state. For example, six weeks in a leg cast means six weeks without working that leg at all, and that means losses in leg muscle size, tone and strength. It also means that you haven't worked on your kicks, footwork and other lower body techniques with that leg. The result is a deficit in both athleticism and skill in the affected areas, and a body imbalance between your recovering areas and your uninjured areas.

So while at this point it is apparent that your injury has basically healed, it is also apparent that you are probably still quite a ways away from being able to do the kind of full-blown, hard-charging workouts that you were used to doing prior to your injury. Just as there is a distinct gap between normal activity and martial arts training, so there is a gap between the athleticism needed for each. This in-between stage is where "posthab" comes in.

Post-rehabilitation, or "posthab," is the term used to describe this unique stage of athletic recovery. It is the regimen of activities that will allow your whole body to work its way back to not only optimal healing, but optimal performance as well. A good posthab regimen will safely close the gap from doctor's release to serious martial arts training and enable you to achieve the following goals:

- reverse the atrophy of the injury-affected areas
- prevent re-injury or further injury
- rebuild athleticism
- regain martial skills and proficiency
- reduce athletic imbalances between the injured and uninjured parts of your body

It is important to proceed in a holistic manner, covering all your bases. You need to address the whole body and the whole workout from recovering areas to uninjured areas, and from warm-up to post-workout recovery in order to achieve your goals.

The posthab part of recovery is of vital importance to the martial artist. This is the last leg of your physical journey to reestablish your pre-injury goals, if possible, and certainly to achieve your own optimal health and wellness as a martial athlete. It is crucial that you intelligently and consistently work a posthab plan that is a broad-based regimen for the most effective recovery possible.

This chapter will cover five areas of posthab focus. It will also discuss how these five areas will improve your strength, cardio and flexibility as well, because your posthab regimen shouldn't just be about picking up the pace and intensity of your workout sessions.

POSTHAB FOR WARM-UP

Since you are coming back to the gym with an athletic deficit in your body, a proper warm-up is now even more important than it was pre-injury. Here are a few benefits of a good posthab warm-up:

- heats up the muscles and increases blood flow and oxygenation to them
- lubricates and hydrates joints to reduce friction and stiffness in tissues that have been out of commission for a while.
- lets the mind as well as the body prepare for what you are about to do in your workout
- shifts metabolism and internal resources away from other functions such as digestion, and redistributes them to the physically active parts of your body
- increases heart rate and respiration gradually, avoiding the shock and strain of starting a workout cold
- locks down the tissues around the affected area through tensing and tightening of muscles and tendons; this adds much needed stability, especially around any joints involved

Go jump rope because it's good for warm-up, cardio, balance, weight loss, muscle tone, coordination, joint lubrication, postural alignment, blood pressure, bone density (osteoporosis prevention/recovery), mental preparation, rhythm and timing, footwork, kicking technique and power.

As a martial artist you are probably familiar with many warm-up exercises. Doing calisthenics, jumping rope, performing gentle kicks and doing forms may be some of the warm-up routines that you are already familiar with. If so, it may be a good idea to start with what you know. Be sure to include a good regimen of gentle stretching in your warm-up. Remember that cold muscles don't stretch very well, so the key word here is *gentle*. (You can find additional warm-up exercises, many targeting specific areas of the body, in Appendix A on page 103.)

From Your Corner:
Mark Graden, Former
NAPMA Director of
Curriculum

Being an instructor, as often happens, I was the odd man out on drills while I was getting my students warmed up and ready for some pretty intense sparring. I wasn't warming up because I was teaching.

I've done this thousands of times in my life, but at 44 years of age, I paid the price. In the third round, when I threw a hook, I hyperextended my elbow causing the bicep tendon to detach and retract.

It was pretty painful, messy, expensive and a big pain in the butt. It really could have been avoided by simply following my own good advice: Warm up before you spar.

POSTHAB FOR THE AFFECTED AREA

The exact site of your injury is probably the focal point of the atrophy you have suffered. Whatever was actually pulled, torn, surgically cut or broken is probably the weakest link in your athleticism. Newly healed tissues may not be completely healed. There may be scar tissue involved or perhaps the surgical removal of tissue has changed the overall dynamic of movement in the injured area. The result is significant weakness in your strength, cardio and flexibility.

Perhaps you have been doing some physical therapy exercises that focus on your injury-affected areas as per your doctor's recommendations. If so, consider including those same therapeutic exercises in your posthab regimen but in more intense forms. You can increase the intensity of exercises by adding more resistance and by raising the number of reps or sets. Maybe you can make those same movements a bit more explosive or intense. After all, if those exercises have brought you back this far, they can probably help you advance farther. At the very least, consider keeping these proven exercises as part of your warm-up routine.

You also want to think about what caused the original injury. What were you doing when you were hurt? Was there a mechanical cause such as catching a knee, being thrown or falling into some equipment? Perhaps there had been warning signs of impending injury such as chronic pain that you ignored or tried to train through.

Some causes may be blatantly obvious, but there may have been other more subtle factors such as poor nutrition, dehydration or lack of a proper warm-up. Things like extra hydration and stretching to help prevent straining a tendon can be just as much a part of posthab as working out with lighter than normal weights. Whatever the causes, adjust your overall plan accordingly, and simply don't do what you were doing when you got hurt.

Be sure to include exercises that target the specific site of your recovering injury and focus the work there. The typical weight machines in a gym are very good for this. For example, if you are using the bicep curl machine properly, the only musculature engaged will be the bicep area. If you are on the leg extension machine, your quad muscles get all the work while your calves and glutes remain unengaged. This will help you focus your workout where it is most needed. It will also help prevent you from trying to workout with too much weight since isolated muscles can't call on other muscles for assistance.

You will notice that atrophied body parts tire quickly, and so you want your posthab regimen to increase not only strength but cardio, as well. This of course means increasing your aerobic endurance in pumping

A postural hold, such as sitting in an invisible chair against the wall, is an excellent exercise for developing muscular tension and overall muscular fitness.

extra blood, oxygen and fuel into the recovering area and pumping waste products out. It also means increasing anaerobic endurance. Anaerobic exercise is short-lasting, high-intensity activity, like sprinting, wherein your body demands more oxygen than is available in your body at the time. Because fighting and self-defense techniques tend to be rapid-burst activities, it only make sense that your posthab routine includes developing your anaerobic threshold again. You need both types of exercises to effectively reverse atrophy and rebuild athleticism in your recovering areas.

POSTHAB FOR THE SUPPORTING AREAS

Remember that the holistic approach to healing means that no part of your body works completely independently of the rest. It makes good sense to get a workout for the areas of your body that are most directly involved with the injured area. For example, a leg with a recovering knee needs a strong calf and powerful quad to help support it. A recovering shoulder needs the added strength of healthy lats, traps and back muscles. So you want to not only strengthen the injured areas but also reintegrate them with rest of body.

The use of free weights is very important for the development of muscle systems and unity. Lifting free weights and keeping them balanced demands the involvement of not only the larger muscles but also many smaller stabilizer muscles that are not engaged when working out on a machine.

Also, remember that your body parts don't work in isolation but together as a unit, even when injured. So your whole body must make allowances for the weakened parts. Consider what happens when you limp. If you have ever hurt your foot or twisted an ankle, you know that it made your whole body walk with a limp. That's because your body intuitively makes allowances for any weakened area so that the whole body can move forward together. The imbalance of injury means that the whole body is out of balance, and so the whole body must work in a unified manner to properly recover.

As you work to recover from an injury, it is important that you avoid as much as possible the imbalances that are common to injury recovery time. The more out of balance you become, the more prone you will be to injury and re-injury.

You can add exercises that are more compound in nature than the isolation exercises used to target the site of injury. Body weight exercises such as push-ups and squats can be incorporated into your routine. Others are dumbbell work and body movement exercises such as calisthenics and martial arts forms. Determine what compound exercises you can include in your regimen that will recruit as many muscles and systems as possible. Examples include burpees, squats, pull-ups, tire flipping and calisthenics. Be sure to address the dimensions of strength, cardio and flexibility.

In terms of lifting weights, remember the differences between isolation machines and free weights. Isolation machines such as bench press and quad curl allow you to focus work on a few specific muscles while using free weights requires you to use strength for stabilizing as well as moving weight. That's why you can bench press more on a machine than with a barbell: All your energy goes into the lift. Athletic health requires the development of stabilizing muscles and the sense of balance that comes with it, which is also key to injury prevention. Be sure to add free weights into your routine so you develop systems and not just specific muscles.

You should also see that everything you do in training has multiple benefits so that you can get the most out of each exercise. For example, in your martial arts training, you have been taught the importance of good technique. One of the reasons is for gaining multiple benefits with every move. For example, let's examine the jab. When you jab, you extend your arm. Offensively, this means extra range for your technique, and defensively, it means you can connect while keeping your head farther away. Rolling your shoulder while jabbing offensively adds power and defensively raises up your shoulder to form a protective pocket for your chin. Now your whole body is rotating into the jab. Offensively, this adds full-body power to the jab, and defensively, it turns your own target areas away from your opponent. You get all that from the simple act of throwing your jab.

In the same manner, look at your posthab regimens with an eye for stacking multiple benefits into everything you do. Work on strengthening an injured area in a manner that is going to prevent further injury at the same time. In your abdominal work and core training, work to also improve back flexibility and trunk movement for both offensive and defensive purposes. When you are regaining your cardio, train the injured and uninjured parts to work smoothly together, improve speed and technique and sharpen your mind as well.

Get imaginative, and set up your training regimen to accomplish the maximum benefit from every activity. A bonus is that having a long list of benefits for each exercise gives you added motivation to stay with your program in the face of pain or boredom.

Four-Count Kick

1-2: Performing your martial arts techniques slowly—like a four-count kick—can be a kind of postural hold.

Having been injured, I've had to work my way back from multiple surgeries that have had me off my training for months. As such, when I'm allowed to begin my training again, I begin with my flexibility to redevelop my range of motion through proprioceptive neuromusclar facilitation or PNF stretching. The contracting and releasing of muscles definitely improves flexibility but also strength. I can't emphasize enough how important I think it is to develop strength throughout your range of motion.

At the same time, I also begin my cardio activity, like jumping rope, swimming, walking and climbing stairs. The intensity depends on my progress.

As my flexibility and cardio improves, I add in strengthening exercises using my body weight in postural holds, like holding planks, sitting against the wall, doing push-ups, etc. After that, I'll add in more dynamic exercises like kettlebells and Olympic-style lifts.

Only after all that, will I begin to move into martial arts techniques that involve impact, like kicking the heavy bag or air shield. Following this format, I was able to regain a full-center split after having my hip resurfaced and been able to participate in kickboxing and Brazilian jiu-jitsu after my ruptured bicep tendon was reattached.

POSTHAB FOR POSTURAL ALIGNMENT

As you probably know from your previous training, proper body alignment is key to good martial arts technique and performance. Much of your power, effectiveness and stability when performing a technique depend on how properly your body is aligned. A good side kick, for example, requires impacting your target at the proper point of leg extension. That proper extension necessitates properly aligning your body from your shoulders to your heel when you kick.

In the same way, it is important that during your reentry to working out, your spine and other body structures are properly aligned in order to increase power and stability overall. This will also help prevent injury, especially those pulls and strains that are inherent with improper technique. Crowded nerves, out-of-place joints, and other results of trauma and prolonged inactivity need to be addressed in your workout. If you spend a lot of recovery time sitting or lying down, consider how that adversely affects your posture.

In your posthab workout, be aware of postural alignment, and put things back where they belong. Establish a good stretching routine to be sure that your bones and tendons are properly aligned before your begin your hard workout. Also be aware of postural alignment when you begin to lift weights. Do a few reps with no weight at all so that your body knows exactly where it is about to be required to go with weights. Concentrate on good form and complete extension in both your resistance training and your body movements. Do your forms with the intent of making each movement as correct as possible, and with great extension.

The disciplines of the martial arts place such large emphasis on proper technique that working on correct alignment should be something that you are already very familiar with. In a posthab setting, just remember that it is now even more important as a means of injury and re-injury prevention, as well as the regaining of martial skills.

POSTHAB FOR SENSE OF BALANCE

Your sense of balance and coordination is like any other learned skill—use it or lose it. If you have been inactive for a period of time due to injury, then your agility and balance have probably suffered atrophy just like your muscles have. In fact, it is your small stabilizing muscles and their fast-twitch response that enables an athlete to exhibit great physical balance. Balancing on one foot for example, requires many small muscles in your lower leg to quickly and strongly contract and adjust. Small muscles like these atrophy through inactivity the same as large muscles and so must be rebuilt not only in areas of strength, but also in speed of response.

Also, your sense of balance begins in the inner ear and like other skills, is dependent on your nervous system to read and interpret sensory data and respond accordingly. Long periods of inactivity such as injury recovery time mean that you haven't exercised those parts of your nervous system any more than you have exercised your muscles. Your sensory awareness of balance, and the physical coordination and agility to react accordingly have atrophied.

In your posthab workouts, be sure to spend some time retraining your sense of balance. You certainly want to avoid trips, stumbles and falls that could cause injury or re-injury. Forms and patterns, standing on one foot, four-count kicks, doing squats while standing on a medicine ball, working with an agility ladder, using a Swiss exercise ball and shadowboxing are some of the exercises you can add to rebuild the attributes of agility, coordination and sense of balance.

POSTHAB FOR SKILLS AND TECHNIQUE

As you increase your workout intensity, you may be very pleased with the speed at which your muscles regain some of their former size and strength. This "muscle memory" cannot only quicken your comeback, but can also give you an added boost of optimism by producing visible results. It can also tempt you to do too much too soon.

You aren't just an athlete. You are a martial athlete. You worked hard to develop and hone the skills and techniques that go with your chosen discipline, so don't let them fall by the wayside. You may have to start at a much lower level of exertion than you were used to before your injury, but that is all the more reason to get an early start on recovering your skills as well as your athleticism. As always, temper your intensity to avoid overexertion.

Remember that there is more affected by injury and atrophy than muscle tissue. The affected tissues include connective tissues such as tendons, ligaments and myofascia. There are blood vessels, nerves, lymphatic elements, cartilage, bones, layers of skin and perhaps other tissues and systems involved. All of these need to be strengthened and conditioned together, and some may bounce back more quickly than others.

Before you try to go back to your pre-injury levels of workout, you must patiently take the time to bring your fitness levels back up in a balanced way. Suppose, for example, that as your recovery has progressed, you have been able to incorporate more and more physical activity. Maybe you have gone from no weight bearing exercises to light weight workouts, or from walking across the room to walking around the block. Now consider adding more calisthenics and body weight exercises before adding heavy weightlifting, or maybe you need to add treadmill and stair-step machine work before you start running on the track.

You may not know what the weakest link is, but your body does and it will work on it. Just be patient and give it time.

From Your Corner:
Danny Dring

When I came back from my hip surgery and started running bleachers, I had no illusions to doing 60 flights the first time. I pushed myself and could have done more on that first day, but I also knew that I was risking catastrophic failure. I could blow out a knee, strain the hip or back or I could stumble and fall from fatigue. I finished tired, but not so exhausted that I couldn't function. I stayed at that level for a week or two and then bumped it up a bit, taking about three months to get back to my peak volume.

From Your Corner:
Bill "Superfoot" Wallace

Many people recovering from a surgery, for example, say, "I've got to make this kick or this punch happen."

No, just go through the same exercises you've gone through your entire life, and let it happen. You have to overcome the trauma of surgery. Maybe some scar tissue has to be broken loose, but it is a mind-set that you need that says, "I can do that again; it will come back. The surgery was an improvement, not an ending."

After all, the surgery is supposed to make you better, isn't it? Then keep reminding yourself that you are going to be better.

POSTHAB PITFALLS

You are excited. You are coming back strong. You are chomping at the bit to recover lost ground, or maybe you are just overjoyed to be able to get back to the kind of serious training that you love. All of this means that you may be tempted to overdo it, which would overwork a still recovering body and put undue stress on tissues and systems that are nominally healed.

Now common sense tells you that you can risk re-injury by doing too much too soon, and the last thing you want to do is cancel out all the time and hard work that has gone into getting you back this far. The results of re-injury can be catastrophic. There can be much more to re-injury than just popping a few stitches.

Another risk of overdoing your workout is additional injury to other areas. Remember that the injured area is connected to other parts of your body in a mutual support system. The threat of injury applies to whole systems and otherwise healthy areas, not just the specific site of your original injury. Consider also that the healthy parts of your body may have been out of commission for a time, and they are not prepared to jump in to the kind of strenuous workout you did before the injury.

Working to exhaustion is a good way to end up with additional injury. What if you drop the weights or lose your grip? What if fatigue slows your reflexes and you fall hard, or don't get out of the way soon enough? The results may be new injuries, new setbacks and the frustration that comes with them.

The body operates as a holistic unit; it will intuitively compensate for a weakened area, and that may put excessive strain on otherwise healthy body parts. For instance, if your right leg is still weak and recovering, your left leg may automatically compensate for it and get a greater-than-expected workout. This additional strain on healthy body parts can lead to additional injury.

Remember also that as an experienced martial artist, you may very well still have the mental and whole-body skills to do many techniques, but your recovering body does not have the athleticism to perform them. Dangers of overworking not only apply to lifting too much weight, but also to skill performance as well.

So be careful. Pace yourself, don't make too great demands on your recovering body and remember that a good workout means everything gets better, not injured or excessively stressed.

You also need to pay close attention to any pain you are experiencing during or after your workout. While the experience of pain should never be used to gauge the seriousness of an injury (as previously discussed in an earlier chapter), it can be used as another tool in setting the level of workout intensity during a posthab session. Some pain is a good thing. For example, a little soreness from yesterday's workout is to be expected and can serve as a welcome reminder that you are getting back to doing what you love. We like to call this the pains of excellence.

Pain can also serve as an important warning sign and give you insights into what is not doing well. Pain experienced from overexertion or overuse tells you that you may need to throttle back a little on workout intensity, or perhaps reduce the amount of weight you are lifting. Pain directly in the site of your injury may be a warning of impending re-injury, or that the wound isn't as completely healed as you thought.

Pain is telling you to be careful and pay attention, so listen to your body. If something hurts, there is a reason. Examine yourself and determine exactly what hurts. Then address the issues that you discover. The smart martial athlete will stay in tune with what the body is saying and wisely use pain as a guide to injury and re-injury prevention.

CHAPTER EIGHT
ACTIVE RECOVERY

The bell rings; end of the round. You go to your corner but not just to kill time. You make the most of your time between rounds. You listen to your corner's instructions, take stock of how you are doing and what you need to do next—rest your body for a bit, get some water and prepare yourself for the next round.

When you have finished your workout session, if all you do is simply stop activity, you will no doubt gain some benefit. But you don't just want to passively recover from your workout; you want to be proactive in the process.

Active recovery is the regimen of activities that addresses your needs at the end of your workout and during the time of rest and inactivity until your next workout. Professional athletes engage in a variety of active recovery therapies immediately after a game or practice session. Even a racehorse is tended to by the trainers at the end of a race who cool him down, walk him out, dry him off and make sure he is ready to go to the stable. That is active recovery. So what should you do after a hard workout? You got it: active recovery.

Suppose you have a good, hard, kicking session and you work your legs to exhaustion. If you just stop activity and do nothing, don't be surprised if you can barely walk the next day. Delayed Onset of Muscle Soreness (DOMS) means your legs will feel fine the rest of the day after your workout, but tomorrow you'll feel like you've been hit by a truck. You can have a great posthab session, giving your recovering areas a complete workout, but if you don't take care of active recovery needs, you may find your recovering injury suffering a setback in terms of swelling, stiffness and pain. So prepare to make the most of your resting time by incorporating these elements into your posthab active recovery regimen.

COOL DOWN

Cool down after a hard workout with some gentle exercises and movement drills. The idea is to let your muscles and metabolism shift gradually from a high level of activity to a low one. In common terms, we don't want to "shock" our bodies with a radical shift from going all-out one minute to inactivity the next. Just like we don't go from zero to 60 without a warm-up period, neither do we go from 60 to zero without a cool-down period.

A hard workout has also left waste products behind in your system. Bits of protein from broken down muscle, lactic acid and other byproducts of metabolism, oxygen depletion and carbon dioxide buildup are just a few of the little nasties that need to be removed from your system. If left in the muscles, they will not do you any favors. So add 10 to 20 minutes of light exercise at the end of your hard workout. This will allow your breathing to recover while keeping your heart rate slightly elevated above your resting rate. This increased heart rate plus moderate body movement results in extra blood circulation that will pump fresh oxygen and nutrients into the muscle tissues, and pump waste products out without producing more. Cool down and give your body an opportunity to move them out immediately after your workout.

Light cardio, treadmill work, doing technical drills and forms are some ways to keep moving and facilitate the cooling down process. To cool down after lifting weights, you can do some of the same exercises you included in your workout, only with much lighter weights or with gentle resistance. Compound exercises such as calisthenics or jumping rope (as mentioned earlier in the Warm-Up section on page 55) and range of motion exercises are some good ways to pump oxygen and nutrition into the muscles and other systems while pumping waste products out. In fact, many of the activities used for warm-up can serve equally as well as transitional exercises for cooling down.

STRETCHING

Range of motion is often limited by a muscle's tendency to contract when stretched to a certain length. That means that it is easier to stretch a fatigued muscle than a fresh one because the muscle's ability to pull back against the stretch has been reduced through fatigue. For example, after a hard kicking session, your fatigued leg muscles will be more easily pulled into a stretch since their strength to resist has been spent on kicking the pads.

That means that while your muscles are fatigued after a hard workout, it is a great time to work on your flexibility as a part of active recovery. In fact, you may find that the most effective stretching is done immediately after your workout. Not only will you see gains in overall flexibility, but also the stretching and releasing of muscles during a stretching session can act like a pump to move blood in and out of tissues, helping to remove waste products. (To learn some cool-down and stretching exercises, see Appendix A on page 103.)

From Your Corner:
Mark Young,
Certified Strength
and Conditioning
Specialist

Recovery time may be the best time for proprioceptive neuromuscular facilitation stretching. PNF stretching operates on the basic notion that if you can get a muscle to contract, you can get it to relax.

For a hamstring, for instance, instead of doing a one-time 15-second stretch hold, you might do a five-second hold, then engage the hamstring as though you were trying to contract the musculature. Then, as you reestablish the stretch, taking the leg back toward the head, you may find it actually goes back farther as you do so.

The cycle of contracting and relaxing is the gist of PNF. You can't force yourself to stretch, but you can force yourself to relax.

This makes stretching very much like a workout, doing sets and reps in order to not only generate force but also to increase range of motion and, in some cases, reduce or eliminate pain.

Talk to the experts on your team to learn more about it.

FLUSHING

Remember the athlete's adage, "Hydrate or die." It takes a lot of water to enable your system to properly move everything it needs to after a workout. Post-workout needs include fuel, oxygen, bio-chemicals of many kinds, blood cells and waste removal to name a few. Because your injured tissues are still in recovery mode, they may have a greater need for all these benefits than before they were injured, so be sure that you replace your fluids as soon as possible after a workout.

How much water do you need to replace? During a workout, your body can absorb about 24 to 32 ounces of water in an hour. However, in hot weather you may lose twice that amount during a strenuous workout. Dehydration can also be an accumulated effect over more than one day, so it is even more important to make sure that you are drinking ample amounts of fluid all throughout the day. A rough estimate would be to drink a typical "bottle" of water (1.2 liter) before your workout, half a bottle every 15 minutes during strenuous exercise, and for post-workout, drink one bottle for each pound of weight lost from workout.

Remember too that as you sweat you lose not only water but also minerals such as sodium, chloride and magnesium. You also burn carbohydrates that must be replaced to maintain energy. This means that water replacement alone may not be enough. A rule of thumb is to drink water to recover from workouts that last under an hour, and perhaps a "sports drink" after longer workouts.

Don't forget that your body is still dealing with the stress of injury and the atrophy of inactivity, so watch yourself closely for any signs of dehydration, and

Caffeine is a diuretic and wrings water from your body's tissues. The cumulative effect of years of drinking coffee, tea, soft drinks, energy drinks, etc., can be chronic mild dehydration. Additional water intake can help offset it and replace the water needed for optimal health and wellness.

For a workout, the rough estimate for water is a typical "bottle" of water (1.2 liter) before, half a bottle every 15 minutes during workout, and a bottle for every pound lost after workout.

stop it early. Symptoms of mild to moderate dehydration include:

- dry mouth
- thirst
- sleepiness or fatigue
- chapped lips
- decreased urine output
- headache
- dizziness
- dark urine

INCREASE BLOOD FLOW

Another way to increase the flow of blood into fatigued tissues and relax tensed muscles is by massage, and although a professional masseuse may be nice, one may not always be available. Don't let that stop you. You can massage many areas of your body with your own hands, and the application of a topical stimulant such as Icy Hot or Tiger Balm can increase effectiveness.

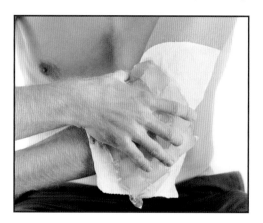

Proper icing takes the heat out of the tissue, causes the blood vessels to constrict and decreases swelling of the iced area. Be careful not to freeze anything—frostbite is not the goal here. Keep something between your skin and the ice, cold pack, or whatever you use, and let the tissues cool down.

Also, the creative use of some simple equipment such as exercise balls can enable you to self-massage other areas. Rolling on a Swiss exercise ball, an eight-inch jelly ball, a tennis ball or even a rolled-up wrist wrap can compress those tissues and help pump blood to them.

After a workout, alternating between cold and hot showers may also help the blood vessels and tissues to dilate and contract, resulting in added blood circulation.

Think about adding Epsom salt (magnesium sulfate) to your bath, too. It is more than just a home remedy for swelling and soreness. Epsom salt is high in magnesium, which is the second most abundant element in human cells. It helps regulate over 325 enzymes and is important for bodily functions such as muscle control, electrical impulses, energy production and waste elimination. Sulfates aid in formation of brain tissue and joint proteins, among other things. Both of these essential substances are readily absorbed through the skin. Add two cups of Epsom salts to your bath and soak for at least 12 minutes.

Rolling up and down against a tennis ball can help gently massage and loosen up a stiff back.

REFUEL

Not only have you exhausted your body's supply of energy during a hard workout, but you have also torn down the tissues and put a strain on many other internal resources. Because newly healed tissues may be more susceptible to damage and depletion than other healthier tissues, this must be addressed with a complete, well-balanced diet.

There is more to meeting your post-workout nutritional needs than drinking a "sports drink" now and eating a good dinner later. In fact, there is a metabolic window of opportunity that occurs immediately after a workout when the body is very efficient at the uptake of protein and other nutrients. A quality protein drink or bar can be an effective way to quickly get much needed nutrition to your depleted system in general and your recovering areas in particular.

Chocolate milk is the poor man's post-workout drink. The milk is a good source of dairy protein, and the chocolate mildly stimulates and releases pleasure chemicals in the brain. Sugars are there for carbohydrate replacement, and the resulting insulin spike will enhance the uptake of nutrients into tissues. It contains calcium, vitamin D for calcium absorption and is affordable and tasty.

Likewise, a carbohydrate drink right after a workout can replenish blood sugar levels and aid in the movement of proteins into muscle tissues. The increased insulin from the carbs will also help with the uptake of nutrients into systems.

Research shows that it usually takes protein an hour or two after consumption to enter the bloodstream and become available to cells. The same is true for most carbohydrates. You can't expect to eat something and have it in your system within just a few minutes. For optimal recovery after your workout, don't put off eating and drinking something nutritious. Your recovering tissues will need it as quickly as you can get it to them.

Remember that a proper diet for healing and recovery means more than eating more protein and less sugar. As our team doctor, Dr. David Klein, says, "The healing process is complicated and can be slowed by a number of processes, including dietary needs. The body must be prepared to heal, and if you don't have all the raw materials in the right combination and proportions, it will take longer to heal."

A "balanced diet" isn't balanced at all unless you add the appropriate micronutrients, including minerals and vitamins. In nutrition, you must restore natural balance. You can't make up for a lack of substance "x" by giving more substance "y." Remember that too much of a good thing becomes a bad thing. So start by restoring the balance of micronutrients, especially the chelated minerals that are missing in our diet. These are necessary for enzyme formation and use. Next, restore the oil balance of fatty acids, and also vitamins. Then diagnostically, you have to look at hormone levels such as testosterone, estrogen, progesterone, DHEA (dehydroepiandrosterone) and insulin levels. Remember that protein and carbohydrates are important, but they don't do anything for you unless the micronutrients are adjusted first.

From Your Corner:
Renegade Coach
John Davies

These supplements are the essentials:

- **Acetyl L-Carnitine:** known for the ability to increase fat metabolism, increase testosterone levels and prevent muscle breakdown
- **Phosphatidylserine:** an incredibly powerful nutrient known to improve cognitive processes such as memory and significantly improve muscular recovery; numerous findings have noted that this supplement can alleviate and support multiple brain functions as well as improve stress management and cortisol reduction
- **Multi-Vitamin:** one that will provide a powerful blend of vitamins and minerals is completely necessary given that the food sources of today have compromised the integrity of soil and nutrients
- **Alpha Lipoic acid (ALA):** 250 mg, twice a day; ALA converts glucose (blood sugar) into energy; it is an antioxidant that neutralizes harmful chemicals known as free radicals, acts as an anti-inflammatory and accelerates muscle recovery
- **Fish oil:** 1-4 grams a day; the omega-3 fatty acids in fish oil decreases triglyceride levels, slows plaque buildup in the blood vessels and slightly lowers your blood pressure; it is also a natural antioxidant
- **Vitamin E:** 400-800 units; another natural antioxidant, it also aids with wound healing, boosts immunity, and can reduce cholesterol and plaque buildup; it is an "essential nutrient," meaning the body cannot produce it on its own
- **Turmeric:** 500-750 mg, twice a day; operates as an analgesic (pain killer) and anti-inflammatory (reduces pain and swelling)

From Your Corner:
Johnny D. Taylor

At age 40, I began to find a lot of gray hairs on my head. Being understandably upset, I researched my problem and discovered that one possible cause was lack of trace elements and minerals in my diet. With nothing to lose and seeing this as a potentially easy fix, I added liquid mineral supplements to my diet, and a month later all the gray was gone. I figured that if minerals were working well on my exterior, they were probably working well on my interior as well, so I've continued taking them ever since.

Today, some 13 years later, it is still working. If I run out of minerals for a couple of weeks, I suffer a noticeable mental fogginess in my thinking, lower energy levels and the return of gray hair. They are my favorite dietary supplements.

If you are in the market, you can find them in liquid form called "colloidal minerals," and they will supply you with trace elements such as copper and selenium that are hard to find in a typical multivitamin. Some are mixed with herbal complexes such as ginkgo and grape seed, and you want to be sure that your chosen brand contains around 72 minerals and trace elements.

Those listed as "chelated" minerals are those elements such as selenium that are bound to an organic substance such as an amino acid, so look for colloidal minerals that come from a vegetative source such as sphagnum moss instead of from inorganic sources such as glaciers, clay or sea beds. The vegetative source may contain more chelated minerals, and probably won't contain significant amounts of heavy metals such as lead and mercury.

CHAPTER NINE
MASTER YOUR EMOTIONS

One moment the fight is going well and you know you are scoring. You feel good. Then something hits you—hard. Your ears are ringing, vision is blurred and balance is going south. Even time seems distorted. Your entire core is frozen in one giant spasm. Your strength drains from your body, and your knees buckle. A hard hit has rocked your world. A long list of feelings and thoughts spin through your mind, and most unpleasant of all, you think: Is it over? Am I done? Can I survive this hit and keep going?

Every fighter knows the importance of having a strong mental game. In fact, anyone can exercise and anyone can play, but the very thing that makes an athlete a fighter is the mental attitude. When you suffer the setback of an injury and tackle the issues of recovery and optimal health and athleticism, you need the kind of strong mental game that will insure your success. Just as your physical plans are well thought out and organized, your mental plans must be as well. That means skills such as educating yourself and redefining your goals are to be applied to your mental game just as they were to your physical regimen. You need to learn to effectively deal with things like emotions and attitude and remain not just an athlete but a fighter. The fight we will tackle here is the onslaught of emotion that can accompany an injury.

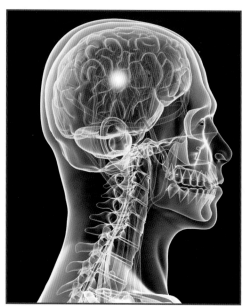

The brain uses 20 percent of your body's energy but makes up only two percent of your body weight.

Ask a room full of people how many of them were in a fight yesterday, and very few hands will go up. Ask a room full of martial artists the same question, and you'll get a different response. Remember that the term "martial" means fighting and warfare, so the idea of pain and injury to the human body is a given. Humanity in general, and in our world in particular, these things happen all the time. As a martial artist you can expect injuries to bring with them all manner of consequences, including emotions.

When your goals are suddenly shoved out of reach, when hard fought gains are lost in a moment, when progress is painfully (literally!) slow, you are going to have an onslaught of many, varied feelings. You are faced with many tough questions: What about my plans and goals? What about my job and income? Can I even tend to my own bodily functions? Is my athletic career seriously impaired or maybe even finished?

How much longer do I have to do this? Is it really doing any good? What's the use of even trying?

Make no mistake, those feelings can be extremely powerful, even overwhelming. In fact, a flood of emotions can do as much to take you out of the fight as an actual injury. Just ask someone who missed a once in a lifetime chance due to a relatively minor injury. Getting back to training can be more of an emotional fight than a physical one.

If you are prepared and if you plan well, then you can greatly enhance your ability to deal effectively with your emotions.

THE SEVEN STAGES OF EMOTION

Dr. Elizabeth Kubler-Ross, a Swedish physician, created the "grief cycle" in the 1960s. The cycle describes seven phases of emotion that we pass through when grieving. Those phases are shock, denial, anger, bargaining, depression, testing and acceptance. However, the cycle has been found to apply not only to imminent loss of life but to other traumas and losses as well. In terms of injury, you'll see how this cycle can play out during your recovery process.

For example, what happens at the moment of injury? You may suffer a mental and emotional shock. The instant you know that something is wrong, that something bad just happened to you, you can mentally freeze in motion. The mind is jerked out of what you were doing and grasps for information about what you are suddenly facing. You may also physically react by turning pale, becoming short of breath or freezing in your tracks.

When shock happens, you may need to sit down and let your body relax while you process what just happened. You may need something or someone to hold onto as your body becomes unstable and your senses go on overload. This is the first wave, but it will pass.

Then what happens? Shock eventually gives way to the reality: You are injured. Your mind probably doesn't like what it learns so it begins to deny what your body is telling you. You may think that this can't happen to you. It isn't real. The pain isn't really that bad; you'll shake it off. Because your mind can quickly realize the enormity of an injury and all its negative repercussions, it will decide you're better off without being injured. Your mind will convince the rest of you that there is no injury.

When you are in denial, you need to be honest with yourself. Remember that you have a long process to work through, and you must not allow yourself to get stuck in any one stage of this cycle. This is the discipline of mind that helps rationality take the place of emotion. As a martial artist, you are used to replacing emotion such as fear and anger with logic and rational thinking. These skills will stand you in good stead when injury strikes and your mind doesn't want to accept the truth.

After denial has been dealt with, reality sets in, and anger arrives. Your natural tendency may be to have a burning fury, or an explosion of anger, and to look for a target to blame. You may become angry at whatever (or whomever) caused the injury, angry at yourself, at the whole situation, at life in general or at any number of other things and people.

Be prepared for anger, and don't let it drive you to do something you will deeply regret later. In the heat of anger, don't allow blame, retaliation and outbursts—both physical and emotional—to make matters worse. Be as angry as you want, but you have to work through it. Don't allow emotional outbursts of anger to make things worse.

When the fires of anger abate, bargaining begins because you are desperate to reverse your circumstances. Maybe it can be easily fixed if only you do thus and such. Maybe there is a unique, even experimental method by which you can turn the situation around in short order. At this point, you are willing to do almost anything to undo what has been done. Again, the rational part of your mind needs to replace the emotions of crazy ideas and irrational actions or deals. It can't be undone, and there is no easy way out. Force yourself again to deal with reality.

But what happens when reality sets in? You might fall into a depression.

Depression is a particularly nasty little monster, and it is a stage where it is all too easy to get stuck or to relapse into. The fact of the matter is that you simply need to understand depression's place in the cycle. It is the sadness that must be worked through in order to get to eventual positive actions. It is the grief over the loss you have incurred due to your injury, and for your own good that grief must be expressed, not bottled up. So grieve, work through the sadness and do all you can to keep moving forward.

Eventually you will come to grips with the truth that you cannot stay in the dark hole of depression forever. Something has got to change. Now you begin to look for realistic things that you can do in your situation. You start to think and move again, and begin a new stage of activity. In the cycle, this stage is called testing.

Testing is a good thing; it means you are on your way back up. You may not have the answers yet, but at least you are moving out of the inactivity and the circular, negative thinking of depression. You are starting to regain some control and are trying out different options for continued improvement of your circumstances.

When you have taken ownership of yourself and your true circumstances, you are finally at the place where you have wanted to get to. Do whatever you can to insure that relapsing is kept to a minimum. Celebrate your arrival to a state of acceptance and whatever hope it holds for you. You have achieved a notable accomplishment, so enjoy it.

This description of the seven stages for a martial athlete on the road to recovery is only one description, but hopefully it will give you a basic understanding of what you are up against emotionally during this time in your life. Of course, every person is different and each injury is unique in its own way. The timeline for each person can vary greatly, with a particular stage or the entire cycle lasting for months or occurring in minutes.

For example, just because you have clawed your way out of depression and into testing, or even acceptance, it doesn't mean that you can't find yourself in relapse, having many of those same feelings again from time to time. As recovery time grows long, it may appear to you as if hard won gains are lost and more opportunities are slipping through your fingers. It's times like these that you may find yourself facing a relapse into a previous stage such as anger or depression. When you are alone with your thoughts and you replay the whole scenario in your mind for the thousandth time, it can drag you down, drag you back.

The temptation to relapse is normal and to be expected. So be prepared with the arsenal of skills already learned and decisions already made that got you through those phases the first time. By the sheer force of your will, refuse to go backward, and press on. After all, you are a martial artist, and quitting isn't an option for you.

SHOCK, the first wave

WHAT HAPPENS: At the moment of injury, you may turn pale, experience shortness of breath and freeze in your tracks.

HOW TO DEAL: Sit or lie down. Let your mind process what just happened.

DENIAL, "this can't be real"

WHAT HAPPENS: Your mind processes a lot of negative information so your mind denies the injury.

HOW TO DEAL: Eventually you must be honest with yourself about the facts. You are injured, and you have a long process of recovery to work through. Let rational thinking replace fantasy.

ANGER, rage against reality

WHAT HAPPENS: As the reality of injury sets in, anger sets in with it. You may experience burning fury, explosive outbursts of anger and targeting someone or something to blame.

HOW TO DEAL: Don't let anger drive you to do something you will regret later. Don't blame or retaliate. Be as angry as you want, but you have to work through it so don't make matters worse.

BARGAINING, "what if ..."

WHAT HAPPENS: You desperately search for ways to reverse your situation. You are willing to try almost anything to undo what has been done.

HOW TO DEAL: Let your rational mind be heard. There is no easy way out, no crazy idea that will work. Force yourself to deal with reality.

STAGE 5 DEPRESSION, hurt and hopeless

WHAT HAPPENS: A greater reality sets in, and you admit to yourself that you are injured. What you are forced to face seems to be all bad and no good.

HOW TO DEAL: Depression is a sadness or grief that must be expressed. Don't bottle it up, but instead mourn your loss and work through the sadness so you can move forward.

STAGE 6 TESTING, moving again

WHAT HAPPENS: You can't stay in the dark hole of depression forever, and something has to change. You begin looking for realistic solutions.

HOW TO DEAL: Testing is good; it means you are active and rational again. You start to regain some control, and try different options.

STAGE 7 ACCEPTANCE, the next phase of life

WHAT HAPPENS: You take ownership of yourself and your situation, and put your circumstances in some semblance of perspective. You are ready to actively pursue your next phase of life.

HOW TO DEAL: This is where you have been wanting to be. Celebrate your arrival to acceptance and whatever hope it holds for you. It's a notable accomplishment.

DEALING WITH DEPRESSION

Because depression is a particularly tough opponent and one that tends to come up quite regularly during the recovery of an injured athlete, we'll spend extra time exploring it.

Depression will rob you of joy and life. It can hinder your healing progress and even rob you of social outlets. Left untreated, depression can lead to counterproductive, even self-destructive behavior. It must not be underestimated in its power to make your recovery time miserable.

Make no mistake; depression must be dealt with decisively through education, preparation and positive action. Fortunately, depression's effects can be recognized and treated so that you can continue on your road to recovery.

So how do you fight depression?

First, don't deny it. Depression can be just as much a part of injury as pain. Expect it, recognize it and deal with it. Denying it is like ignoring a wound: It will only grow worse.

Second, take responsibility for the fact that you are depressed. Ultimately you are responsible for your health and wellness. At the end of the day, it is your injury, your recovery and your fight against depression. So go on the attack, and proactively put together your plan for dealing with this evil.

Third, don't quit. How many times have you learned to never quit and never give up in your training? Depression may set up a long-term siege against you, so you must be mentally prepared for a long battle. Make up your mind that you will not quit. You will not succumb to the darkness and despair of depression. You will fight until you have decidedly won.

Fourth, as you learned in Chapter 5, it's time to redefine your goals. This time though, redefine your mental goals. The fight changed when you became injured, and so you must set new and appropriate goals for yourself. It is through setting and achieving goals that positive, visible, measurable progress is made, and that includes your fight against depression.

Fifth, educate yourself. Just as your particular injury needs to be studied and understood, so does your particular struggle against depression. What are the symptoms? Is there a person in your life who knows you well and can act as your "early warning system?" Can your medical professionals assist you? (This of course necessi-

Depression

Depression can produce a wide range of symptoms, not just "being depressed." During injury recovery it is important that you recognize depression when it appears. Here are some of the noticeable symptoms of depression. Check yourself as objectively as you can, and consider asking a trusted friend to also watch you for these symptoms:

- **loss of interest in daily life**
- **hopelessness and pessimism**
- **problems sleeping**
- **difficulty focusing and/or concentrating**
- **unexplained weight gain or loss**
- **easily annoyed and irritable**
- **chronic fatigue**
- **low self-esteem**
- **loss of sex drive**
- **unexplained physical symptoms such as back pain or headache**

Regular exercise is enjoyable because it causes your body to produce mood-elevating chemicals known as endorphins. These natural opiates that give you a sense of joy and optimism are commonly known as the "runner's high." Over time, you become "addicted" to these compounds, and you get antsy when your workout routine is disrupted. When injury strikes and you are taken out of the routine of regular workouts, your body may suffer endorphin withdrawal. Without its regular dose of mood-elevating compounds, you can slip into depression.

tates that you talk openly and honestly to them about your struggle against depression.)

Sixth, exercise. Creative cross-training can get you busy again. Don't worry about what you cannot do; focus on what you can do, then do it! The act of exercising, regardless of how unimpressive it may appear, can help you feel as if you are taking back some control over your life. Remember those lovely endorphins? See if you can get them back through some exercise. Their very job is to brighten your mood. Don't overdo it, but do it!

Seventh, *laugh*. Like the proverb

says: "A merry heart does good like a medicine." Those same mood-elevating chemicals you get from exercise can also be released through laughter. So find what makes you laugh and enjoy.

Finally, reevaluate your life. Everyone should reevaluate his or her life and priorities from time to time; that's just good sense for living. So if an injury is forcing you to ask yourself the hard questions, then make the most of your downtime to reestablish exactly who you are, what you are about and what you intend to do with your one and only life. It may be that an injury is a blessing in disguise, forcing you to deal with large life issues that you have been too busy to address. Are you more than your martial athletic ability? Is there more to you than this injury? The results of your personal soul searching, reprioritizing and self-evaluation may be some of the best things that come out of your downtime.

**From Your Corner:
Danny Dring**

After rupturing my bicep tendon, I had a commitment to a BJJ seminar at a camp. I focused on teaching things that didn't involve my arms, such as leg techniques in grappling.

In telling people about my injury, I would tell them that it was only a speed bump in the grand scheme of things. I still had my health, could still run, kick, stretch and a ton of other things, even with a hurt arm.

"I'll be back," I said, "It's not the end of my career; it's just a challenge."

Now, I was not so cavalier the day the injury happened. In the blink of an eye, my plans were all thrown out the window. I knew that this thing hurt, was going to be expensive, difficult and take a lot of time and attention to heal.

I verbalized my feelings and my "anchor points" of faith in my ability to heal. I told myself I would overcome this, and that I was coming back. I thought: I AM going to be fine; I AM going to continue to train.

I hammered that into my mind, vocalized it, wrote it down, repeated it to others and kept it in front of me. It became a self-fulfilling prophecy because I did come back.

Sometimes that is the tricky part: finding ways to keep your goals in front of you, keep them important and worthwhile, and keep your confidence and faith in your ability to achieve those goals. It must be something that you are very interested in accomplishing.

POSITIVE MENTAL ATTITUDE

You have learned how to conquer the emotional deficit of a negative attitude, which takes you back up to neutral "ground zero" on the attitude scale. However being passive, neutral or noncommittal is not an option. It's time now to build on that and bring your attitude up the scale from zero into the positive range. You must move forward aggressively in your mind. You need strong optimism, and that is what a positive mental attitude is about.

The great thing about attitude is that you are perfectly capable of choosing any one you want. In fact, whatever attitude you have is the direct result of choices you have made in your mind and life. Whether you are aware of it or not, you are always choosing your attitude.

Mental Attitude Scale

Negatives				Neutral				Positives
Shock	Depression	Denial	Anger	Acceptance	Faith	Determination	Inspiration	Optimism

Attitude is the result of what you dwell on in your mind. If you dwell on all the bad things that happen in life, you become a pessimist with a negative attitude. If you dwell on the good things that come your way, you become an optimist with a positive mental attitude (PMA). Because you can choose what you think about, you can choose your attitude. That means all the healing benefits of a PMA are yours for the taking. Fortunately, there are always positives where negatives appear.

Are you in pain? That means you are still alive. Are you hobbling along, barely able to move? That means you can move. Are you able to dwell on your misfortune? That means you still have your mind. Are you sick of your bed or couch? That means you are not homeless. Is the healing process progressing slowly? That means it is progressing. Is it bad? Then it could be worse.

Now, lest you think this all sounds like so much Pollyanna, feel-good fluff, consider a few reasons to work on your PMA: First, if it is possible for you to choose being positive over being negative, you owe it to yourself to do it for your own state of mind and for those who have to put up with you. Second, your body is always responding to your mind and it will respond to what you think about all the time, to what you tell it. Tell it good things, and your body will do good things. Tell it bad things, and bad things will occur. The idea is that you become what you think about all the time. So ask yourself questions such as these in as positive a manner as you can:

- What do you think is going to happen to you?
- What do you think you are going to accomplish?
- What do you believe the future holds for you?
- How much faith do you have in your ability to recover?

Because your mind is such a powerful thing and controls so much that goes on in your body and your life, your answers to these questions can determine to a large degree how well you recover.

Remember too that it is a truth of life that a person usually finds what they look for. Look for fault and you will find it. Look for the bad in life, and you will see it everywhere. But look for the good, the positive, the beneficial and you will find that as well. If you choose to look for healing, health and wellness, you will find plenty of ways and means to optimize your recovery.

From Your Corner: Mark Graden, Former NAPMA Director of Curriculum

When I was young I had a lot of back injuries, and it gave me the mentality of having a "bad back." I thought that things were always going to be like that, that I would always have to be careful not to lift things, and that I would have trouble with something like karate. This was really a false and negative mind-set to be in.

Then a therapy trainer taught me that the vast majority of injuries that you are going to have you could either preempt or fix yourself. Proper conditioning, core conditioning, proper warm-up and knowing how and when to stretch taught me an approach that made a huge difference in my mind-set.

That was a total flip-flop for me because it wasn't negative. I didn't have a "bad back" after all, and I wasn't restricted by all those limitations that were in my mind before.

With the old mind-set, I wouldn't play volleyball with my students because someone had told me my fifth and sixth lumbar were "out," whatever that means. Once I was properly taught and trained, however, I learned that if something really screwed up, I was going to know it. If I had pains, I was probably going to be able to work through them.

I went from having a disempowered mind-set to one that is really empowered. In fact, I didn't have a single injury that I couldn't take care of myself from 1983 until 2008, when I ruptured my bicep tendon.

INSPIRATION

One of the cornerstones of a PMA is your ability to be inspired. Think of all those inspirational stories you have heard in your life. They captured your attention, pointed you toward role models and fired your imagination with encouragement and enthusiasm. They were probably all about people who overcame the negatives in their lives, and it took their positive mental attitude to do it. For the sake of your recovery, you can intentionally seek to be inspired.

Inspiration is that invisible strength and encouragement that comes from seeing what is possible while ignoring what is probable. It focuses the martial athlete on striving for the greatest possible success, overcoming seemingly impossible odds and obstacles along the way.

Without inspiration, the work of recovery falls into drudgery and breeds unhappiness and discontent, and that bad attitude leads to failure. A person who is inspired will be much more apt to continue progressing toward lofty and worthwhile goals, leaving a trail of defeated obstacles behind him.

It is incredible what the human being can overcome. There are stories of a myriad of martial athletes in all areas of endeavor who have overcome great tragedy, including extreme injury. Everything from car and motorcycle wrecks, broken bones, fight injuries and freak accidents, to injuries incurred in the line of duty by law enforcement and military personnel have sidelined these martial athletes for a time. Many were able to overcome these setbacks, maintain or regain a sense of athleticism and regain mobility. They were able to also maintain a sense of dignity and self-worth through the process.

Look around and you will find that the world of martial arts is full of worthy role models.

Are you faced with aging to the point of being unable to "come back?" Every active martial artist in the world that is older than you is apparently finding ways to stay in the fight. Why not you?

Have you suffered a physical devastation? How many people can you find that have lost even more than you have, yet they are still in the fight? If they can do it, so can you.

This book contains stories of martial artists from many backgrounds who have overcome injury. Their stories are not included just to make a more interesting book, but to inspire you and to convince you that it can be done. Their testimonials stand as proof that victory is within your reach. If others can do it, then so can you.

Has there ever been anyone with a situation similar to yours who overcame it? Have any others defeated the kind of opponent you now face? Are there role models and heroes who can inspire, motivate and keep you convinced that you can do this, too? Then find them. Hear their stories and let their positive experiences inspire you toward your own greatest achievements.

You can also find inspiration in your own experiences and accomplishments. Just as it is impressive what others can come back from, it is also amazing what you can come back from. A deep-seated belief in yourself and your ability to heal will go a long way in keeping you inspired and on track toward optimal health and wellness. That self-generated inspiration will assist in maintaining your PMA and the faith necessary to achieve your goals, and will motivate you to keep on keeping on.

Having your own plan can also inspire you. If just reading this book has improved your optimism and increased your level of inspiration, then you have already made some progress. Now build on that progress by being careful to complete the Fightsheets that are included at the end of the book. (See page 125.) Just having this plan of attack will bolster your enthusiasm and inspiration. Your own progress can inspire you as well. When you first get back to working out after an injury, the sheer volume of what you cannot do may seem overwhelming. There are things that you can do though, and those are the things that are important. So focus on what is possible today.

Also, set the never-ending quest for improvement as a goal. You know what you can do, so how can you make it better? How can you improve, excel, refine? Keeping your focus on the possibilities that are before you can go a long way in maintaining a positive attitude, and in keeping up your level of inspiration. You know progress when you see it, and as you see yourself growing in levels of athleticism, let it inspire you. No matter if your situation seems dire or your circumstances extreme. No matter if you seem to be inching along when you would rather sprint. Progress is progress, so don't minimize it. Maximize it, and let it inspire you.

One last thing: Remember the people whose stories inspire you? They probably never set out to be such inspirations. They just really wanted to improve their lot in life, get through some really tough times and get back to what they loved doing. Consider that if they can stay in the fight and inspire you, then you can stay in the fight and inspire others. Now it is your turn to be inspirational. Choose a PMA and live a good story for yourself and others.

From Your Corner:
Joe Lewis

My specialty is that I know how to stay motivated. I do it by seeking inspiration. Motivation is like your emotional quick fix; it lasts for a day or so, then it's gone. Inspiration lasts a lifetime. You've got to find things that inspire you daily, and that is more than just going up in rank. You've got to find what stirs your passion. Get in touch with that deep part of you, your sacred core, and find what inspires you there.

From Your Corner:
Danny Dring

Passion is one of the things I'm drawn to that keeps me going. After having suffered from injury that made me wonder if I would ever be able to do what I want to do again, that love of performing my martial arts makes every day a gift from God. I feel fortunate because I saw my flexibility go away, along with my ability to do certain techniques.

Now, every time I run bleachers, lift weights, have a great workout, kick the Thai pads or whatever, I'm fired up just to get to move! I'm back in touch with that joy of being able to perform, and that passion, that love, for what I do is inspiration for me.

CHAPTER TEN
FROM VISION TO REALITY

*You are back up, but the ring is still spinning. You circle your opponent,
shake your head to clear the cobwebs and strain to focus. In your mind's eye,
you see yourself landing the combination that your opponent is susceptible to.
You imagine him hitting the mat and see the referee holding up your hand.
The mental images are so clear, it's as though you were already holding the trophy.
You are absolutely determined to see this thing to the end, no matter how many rounds
and no matter what the final outcome may be.*

Once you've latched onto a positive mental attitude and inspiration about what you can accomplish in recovery, it's time to forge those ideals into something more personal and specific. It's time to develop and pursue your ultimate vision.

Vision is defined as a clear mental image of a preferred future, and it is a necessity for anyone looking to make the most of any journey in life. Not just for the corporate boardroom or the artist's studio, vision also helps the recovering martial athlete know where he is going, how he will get there and what it will be like when he arrives. You must get a clear picture, a vision, of your ultimate destination.

For our purposes, that destination is your optimal recovery to health and wellness. Having this clear vision of yourself in an optimized state of athleticism is indispensable to a comprehensive plan for your restoration to health. Without this sense of destination, you wander aimlessly. With it, you can redefine your goals, plot a course to achieve them, mark your progress and arrive at the destination of your own choosing in the shortest amount of time possible.

Start by taking the raw materials of a strong positive mental attitude and imagine what you want your life and body to look like when you are all healed up and returned to your greatest possible state of health and wellness. Build the image in your imagination of what you will be doing, of the accomplishments you will have achieved and of the gains you will have made. See yourself in your imagination fighting, running, working out, training, competing and winning. See yourself with the maximum possible healing and restoration to health.

The good thing about the imagination is that it is just as easy to imagine something great as it is to imagine something mediocre. So build your mental image according to what you think is possible, whether it seems probable or not. This is key: Your mental picture of a desired future should strain the realm of possibility, being neither set too low as to be modest and uninspiring nor being set so high as to be completely impossible to achieve. You want to set your preferred future at such a level so as to get the maximum inspiration from it, while still being capable of having faith that it can become your reality and your actual future.

Now you have your "destination," the future that gives you the best imaginable outcome for your health, healing and martial arts career. Revisit it in your mind often. You must keep this vision in front of you, reminding yourself every day, or perhaps several times each day, that this is where you are headed.

Now it is time for some exercises and methods to make your vision a reality. You will use inner resources through a technique known as visualization, and you'll use outer resources through your physical senses.

MAKE YOUR VISION REAL THROUGH VISUALIZATION

Let's begin with visualization. Sometimes shrouded in mysticism, visualization is found in Eastern religions, New Age activities, professional sports training and biofeedback. Even the Bible speaks of meditation and inner vision. For our purposes, we'll speak of visualization as the mental exercise of training your brain, especially the subconscious mind, to believe and to do whatever you consciously desire. What you desire is for your grand vision to become a reality.

In athletics, this is sometimes called "mental rehearsal." It is the quarterback who mentally sees himself throw the perfect pass or receive an enormous trophy. It is the Olympic ice skater visualizing herself landing three double jumps or standing on the podium for her gold medal. It is the martial artist seeing himself in his mind's eye throw a powerful palm heel, break all his boards at testing and have his *sensei* tie a black belt around his waist. In the area of injury recovery, it is the mental process of seeing the efforts of a great performance in terms of healing and renewed wellness. The power of visualization can be used not only for pursuing your ultimate vision of maximum overall athleticism but also for the specific activities of healing.

Without visualization, your body will still want to heal. It wants to lay down calcium, knit tissues back together, reroute or reconnect nerve endings and a wide variety of other wondrous things. However, like water running downhill, the body left to itself will only heal in its own natural time. Visualization is like adding a pump; the water still goes downhill but more efficiently, at a faster rate and in a manner that is determined by more than just gravity. Visualization adds elements of control, efficiency and speed to the recovery process. It can help the body lay down calcium more efficiently, knit tissues back together more quickly, reconnect nerve endings with more intention and give you a sense of optimism through being proactive. It's a wellness pump for your brain.

How the process actually works is a matter of much speculation, but martial athletes are not as much concerned with how it works, as they are that it works. Consider that everything your body does, it does because your mind tells it to. Whether consciously, subconsciously or unconsciously, the commands come from your mind to walk, breathe, speak, see, dream, dilate blood vessels, regulate body temperature and blood pressure, eat a steak, watch a movie … the list goes on and on. It is not that big a stretch to understand then that the mind (especially the subconscious mind) controls the methods, rates and details of healing, health, wellness and recovery.

In order to use the power of visualization you need to learn the mechanics of how your mind works to bring about the realization of your vision of recovery. The key is putting your subconscious mind to work.

Your subconscious mind is in charge of healing your body. It determines resource allocation, manages all physical systems, regulates blood flow, resting/waking cycles, etc. Like a supercomputer, it handles thousands of activities at a time, accomplishing all of them according to how it is programmed. Fortunately, you also have the capability of reprogramming your subconscious mind to carry out your conscious wishes, including the healing processes. It is important to know that because your subconscious mind isn't "conscious," it doesn't know or care if what you tell it is true or false, real or imagined, present or future. Like any good computer, it just accepts the programming you give it and acts accordingly.

There are three parts of your conscious mind that you are going to learn to use to program your subconscious for optimal healing. First, you will engage your logic and intellect, located in the left side of your brain. You already used this intellectual side when you educated yourself about your injury, when you built your regimen for the six dimensions of athletic health and logically plotted your road to recovery.

Next, you will engage your creative imagination located in the right side of your brain. This is composed of all the images and possibilities you hold in your mind, especially the ultimate destination of your vision. You already used this imaginative side when negative emotions that accompanied your injury made you imagine how bad your life might become. You also use it each time you redefine your goals and when you build a mental picture of your grand vision of optimized athleticism.

Last, you will engage your passion located in your midbrain. Of course, you are very familiar with a wide range of emotions, but it is the emotion of passion that is most important here. Passion is an absolute must if you are going to see your vision become reality. You must emotionalize your vision and set it on fire! Only emotion such as passion generated from the midbrain can connect the logical left side of your mind together with the creative right side. You need the active participation of all your mental faculties in order to achieve optimal recovery. You've got a great vision, but how passionately do you want it? You've got to want very strongly to heal and recover, and that passionate desire for making the greatest possible comeback must burn clearly and brightly in your conscious mind in order for your vision to become a reality.

Also, recovering from an injury can be a long, tough and painful ordeal, and you will need the drive and determination that only passion can give. When people make commitments, expend great resources and stay on track for something as important as optimal injury recovery, it isn't just for what they know through logic or for what they can dream creatively. It is for *what they love*. They do it for passion! Only a vision that is fired with passion will keep you going should your recovery become difficult and slow. Your passion for recovery and athleticism must outweigh all the work, setbacks, pain, distress, frustration and everything else that tries to hinder progress toward your vision. Only if your internal scales tip in favor of your passionate desire will you continue on your quest. Otherwise you will settle for minimal healing and mediocrity of life.

Do the same thing at the same time every day for two weeks and you will build a habit. Do it for 30 days, and you'll build a habit that is hard to break.

Now it is time to get to the actual exercise of visualization. First you will need a quiet place and time to relax. Just before going to sleep at night or perhaps during a daily quiet time in the afternoon (or both) make great times to practice and improve your visualization skills. Perhaps the best time for you is while you are taking a power nap, or when you go to therapy and have to lie still for a while, or when you lie at home under ice or heat. Remember that you want to build a habit of visualization so pick a time and place that you can do it consistently. You may have to actually schedule a time as an appointment for yourself.

Now relax and breathe deeply. Begin by shutting down all the many things your mind is busy doing. Focus on building in your imagination the specific images you want to represent your healing. If you have done your homework, you know the details of the healing process that your recovery requires. For instance, you know the bones or muscle fibers that need to mend back together. So in your imagination, "see" the specific recovering area and imagine all the necessary elements of healing flow in and accomplish their job. "See" the healthy flow of blood and oxygen, a flood of nutrients and wellness or anything else that represents the healing and wellness you desire.

You may not have to be all that technical with your visualization imaginings. Some people have effectively visualized little workers in hard hats who carry shovels and tools down to the injured area to repair it. That's the interesting thing about the subconscious mind—it doesn't care if something is real or not. It just interprets whatever information it is given and acts accordingly. Still, for many (including the authors of this book), something that deals a bit more with the physiology of the body seems to work better. That's why we educate ourselves about the injury involved: to engage the logical and intellectual power of the left brain, the imagination and creativity of the right brain and the passion and emotion of the midbrain. In doing so, you may find that you are able to visualize as closely as possible what actually needs to take place in an injured area. The idea is to train your subconscious mind to work hard and effectively in the specifics of the healing process.

Once you are visualizing the healing process, hold those images in your mind for several minutes. In your mind, tell yourself what you want to be true and not how injured you are. Because the subconscious mind doesn't distinguish between fact and fiction, tell yourself what you are "seeing" in your imagination—that you are healing, that you are getting better, that injury and weakness are flowing out and that health and wellness are flowing in. Tell yourself that oxygenated blood is flowing into the area, carrying everything needed for perfect healing and carrying away all toxins and waste products. Then tell yourself how great it feels to be healing. Experience in your mind the passionate positive emotions of joy and thankfulness that you are healing and life is improving all the time. Tell yourself how happy you are to be moving toward health and wellness and how excited it feels to return to training and whatever else makes you happy. Go ahead. Shoot for the moon. Your subconscious mind will believe anything you tell it, accept your programming and act accordingly.

Your objective in visualization is to build a strong belief system in your own ability to heal and recover. You want to construct a deep-seated positive mind-set about your healing. You want to develop an unshakable faith that you can and will get better. You want to convince yourself that healing is going on in a positive way. You want to strengthen your conviction that you are actually getting better. You want to eliminate all the negatives in your thinking and replace them with positives. Mind, body and spirit— you are programming yourself for success instead of failure.

The end result is that you can honestly say, "I am getting better," because it will be the truth. Your subconscious mind will work day and night to make your inner vision of physical healing a reality, and even if the only benefits are an improved mood and optimism, visualization will be worth the effort.

It is very important to understand that the subconscious mind is programmed by repetition, not by logic. That is why you can drive a car without "thinking about it." You have driven so much that it happens "automatically." The same thing happens when you are training in your martial arts. You can execute a good technique with all its complexities and nuances, even though you are concentrating on your training partner or opponent. That's because you have drilled and practiced technique properly. The training takes over, and you do it without having to think about all the details involved.

Now, concerning your visualization exercises, the same principle applies. It is through repetition that you reprogram and train your subconscious mind to achieve your desired results. You must be consistent with these exercises, performing them faithfully every day, preferably more than once. This is how you program your subconscious mind over time to get better and better at sending healing, nutrients, oxygen, health, wellness and all things positive to any and all areas that need it. Through repetition, it will grow to believe all this is true and will act accordingly to make it all happen, giving you positive feedback in the form of help, health and healing.

This process can significantly speed and optimize the healing process, elevate your mood, give you a sense of being proactive and regaining a sense of control over the whole recovery process. Your faith in your ability to heal will be bolstered. Your body's ability to heal itself will be optimized. You will become more aware of what your body needs to make this maximized process happen. You may literally think yourself back toward health.

One of the great benefits of programming yourself through repetition is that repetition also forms habits. We humans are creatures of habit, and that tendency can be harnessed and used for our benefit. Do the same thing at the same time every day for two weeks and you will have formed a basic habit. If you do it for 30 days, you will have formed a habit that is hard to break. Because the repetition of good things forms good habits, you can use the power of habit to make the journey to your visionary destination almost automatic. If through repetition, you can build a strong habit, then you can replace the need for motivation and self-discipline with the internal drive of that habit.

For example, instead of trying to stay motivated to do your therapy for six months, you can focus on making it an absolute daily event for two weeks, then reset your goal for the completion of 30 uninterrupted days. After that, your innate sense of habit will help drive you to continue. Instead of having to "make yourself" do your therapy, you will feel the urge to do what you have been doing, when you have been doing it and the way you have been doing it for the last month. You have now effectively reduced the need for self-discipline from six months down to 15 days. Your sense of habit takes over from there, creating and strengthening the desire and drive inside you, to help you reach your goal.

Remember that in your daily visualizations, you can visualize not only the physical healing processes you desire but just as easily and effectively visualize the personal characteristics you wish to develop. So use the same techniques to see and feel yourself as the passionate, determined, persistent, victorious and well-adjusted martial artist that you are.

Visualization is a process available to anyone who wants to apply it. It is also a learnable skill; don't be discouraged if the process seems odd or doesn't seem to work very well at first. After all, when you first began your martial arts training, it also seemed odd and didn't work very well. There is much information in other books and on the

Internet about different techniques, methods, tips, etc., on the subject of visualization. Find what works for you and develop your skills.

Back in 1988, I was having some real difficulties with my back and staying in top shape while competing in a national fight circuit became more difficult because of these issues.

One day I sneezed. That sneeze ruptured my L4/L5 and L5/S1 discs. It also blew a piece of disc out onto a nerve root. It was the most horrific pain I have ever been in, and it dropped me in my tracks. It felt like someone shoved electrodes into my back, causing spasms that looked like gophers running up and down my back. The phone was only the length of the couch away, but it took me twenty minutes to reach it and call for help. The doctors used muscle relaxers as temporary help, but I continued to have trouble walking, had an "absent foot reflex," and experienced muscle atrophy in my calf and foot. I was pretty much told by a neurosurgeon that I would have to have back surgery.

I started doing my research on this injury and the options for treatment. I discovered there are five fundamental reasons why people have back surgery: loss of bowel control, loss of bladder control, loss of sexual function, muscular atrophy and pain management. The vast majority was for pain management. The problem was that ten years down the road, there was no appreciable difference between those who had surgery and those who didn't in terms of pain management. Because pain management was my chief issue, these statistics were a bit disappointing. Also, when the surgeon explained the operation to me, how they would cut through the muscles of my back, that I would only be able to lift this much weight and that I would no longer be able to do this or that … . That convinced me that I wanted to avoid surgery if at all possible. So I began to look at all other treatment methods I could find.

I had physical therapy, traction and interferential treatment. I also did a lot of visualization. I used a self-hypnosis tape to help me reach a profound state of being relaxed. I would visualize watching a movie screen where I would be going down an escalator, counting backwards, and hit the bottom at a state of relaxation where I could really zone out and get in tune with my body. I would visualize my body with a healing aura around it. I had studied the MRI scans and X-rays. I had listened to doctor explain, "This is the bulge, and this is what needs to happen to it." I would picture that bulge shrinking and being pulled back in. I was able to see myself getting better and put a strong, positive picture of that healing in the forefront of my mind and in my subconscious mind, as well. I would work on my deep breathing, seeing myself breathe all the way into those muscles, gathering the pain and exhaling it out. I would also tell myself positive affirmations:

- "I am getting better."
- "I am healing."
- "I am getting ready to resume activities."

Those are very powerful affirmations and have a profound effect on the mind and body.

At bedtime, I would tell myself that sleep time is a time for healing. I would focus on the positive and see myself getting better. That's how I went to sleep every night. When I woke up the next morning I felt like I had just spent the last seven to nine hours actually doing something that was allowing me to heal.

Every day, I would "see" myself getting better, and every day I would bolster my faith and build a certainty of belief in my ability to heal from this thing, that I would not lose to it, and that I would not have to undergo surgery. This also gave me a sense of being proactive, of taking positive action and being involved in my healing. I worked at it, including it as part of my regimen along with stretches, ab work, pelvic tucks and other exercises.

It worked because my foot reflex came back, which shocked some people, and most of the atrophy was reversed. In 1989, I went on to win the men's third- and fourth-degree black-belt divisions in the United States Taekwondo Federation tournament circuit, getting points for form and fighting. I was runner up in 1990, and I won it in '91, '92 and '93. I was the first person to be a four-time national champion for the tournament circuit.

Visualization played a huge part in allowing me to not only come back, but to excel at what I did. It has worked wonders for me through hip surgery, bicep tendon rupture, knee surgery and many other injuries. Was it the sole reason for my recovery? No. I was diligent in my nutrition, hydration and rest. I had educated myself about what was possible and knew my parameters. I had armed myself. But knowing that I could come back was extremely important, and much of that confidence came through regular visualization.

MAKE YOUR VISION REAL THROUGH SENSORY INPUT

Other ways to program your mind to make your ultimate vision a reality is through the power of your senses. We experience life through our senses. All that we see, hear, feel, taste and smell make up our perception of the world. So if you maximize the programming of your subconscious mind, you will need to give it sensory input. That means that rather than just thinking good thoughts, dwelling on the positives and visualizing in your mind, you need to physically see, hear and experience your vision becoming real.

You must keep your visionary goals in front of you. It is necessary to be constantly reminded of what has become important so that the fire of desire stays kindled. Do this by finding pictures that represent your vision to you. They are reminders of what is important and what rewards await you upon reaching your goals. Any number of other things can convey a positive source of motivation and desire. Post these around your world where you will see them often. These images will act as visual reminders of the mission you are on.

Also, write your ultimate vision, your visualization exercises and other positive affirmations down on paper. Add plenty of detail and description and make it as real on paper as in your imagination as you can. This is another way to make your mental desires tangible because you've translated them from thought into writing. Once you have it down on paper, read it to yourself, preferably aloud, every day. Now you can "see" your goals in your mind, in pictures and on paper.

Next, find icons of your vision. An icon is a small object that carries a great deal of meaning. A cross is an icon of Christianity. A black belt is an icon of martial arts. A dollar sign is an icon for money. What can you use as an icon for your recovery? What small item and action can you use in your daily life to represent what is impor-

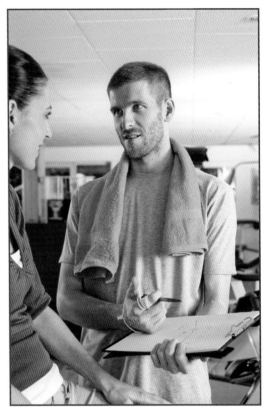

You need authorities and peers to help reinforce your progress toward a vision of optimal health. You may find these positive influences already in your corner.

tant to you? Perhaps you can hang your favorite workout shirt or your black belt on your doorknob so that every time you open the door, you see and touch your icon. Find a few items that represent to you the best of what you desire and are working toward, and place them strategically around your world. It is also important that you interact with them in some way. It then becomes a constant reminder of the road to recovery that you are on.

Save your pennies toward a special purchase to celebrate the reaching of a specific goal. Perhaps you can keep a wrist wrap or boxing glove on the seat of your commode. Every time you move it out of the way, you will be reminded that you are coming back. Have you finished your prescription pills or a bottle of vitamins? Leave the empty bottles sitting upside down where you can see them and view them as proof of progress. Get a calendar and post your recovery schedule on it. Keep tally of days that you have done what you are supposed to do, marking off the days until a goal is reached. Let the sight of the growing number of tally marks be a constant source of encouragement to you as you see tangible proof of your progress toward the goals of your desire.

Now that you have decided what you want your body to do in terms of health, healing, wellness and attitude, start telling yourself that it is happening. Remember that your subconscious only cares about what you tell it repeatedly. So tell yourself you are healing. Tell yourself you are getting better all the time. Tell yourself that your future is bright, you don't quit and that you are defeating this opponent called injury. Tell yourself these things often, regularly and with as much conviction, passion and emotion that you can muster. You will be pleasantly amazed at what your mind can accomplish in your body when your chosen belief system takes over.

Self-talk or self-coaching can be a huge asset in your quest for optimal healing. You can use it to turn your competitive nature to your favor as you encourage and spur yourself on in your fight for recovery and the overcoming of obstacles. So give yourself verbal affirmations repeatedly. Convince yourself that they are real so that your subconscious mind will begin to believe them and take appropriate action in your body. Be sure to coach yourself in positive ways; you'll see your body respond positively. That means no blaming or browbeating yourself (or others) for your less than stellar circumstances. You've taken ownership and responsibility for your own healing. You've chosen your positive attitude. Now hammer it into your brain using your own words.

Remember that of all the voices that you hear, the most influential one is your own. That's why it is important that your self-talk is audible. At the same time, always be careful what you tell yourself, because you will believe it on a very deep level and your whole being will respond accordingly. So make a conscious decision to look for the good, dwell on it and speak it to yourself with passion. As you do your self-coaching exercises, you'll hear your recovery goals being spoken in the most influential voice you know—your own.

In the same vein, make a list of "I am" statements that reflect how you want to be true to yourself and your healing. Make them as positive and affirming as you can. Write down as many as you want and read them to yourself at least once every day. These may be similar to what you see and tell yourself mentally during your visualization times.

Do you want to feel better? Then say to yourself, "I am feeling better." Do you want to see improvement in your range of motion? Then say to yourself, "I am seeing improvement in my range of motion." Do you want to develop the characteristic of persistence? Then tell yourself, "I am developing the characteristic of persistence." You get the idea.

You can also reinforce your progress toward your vision by experiencing the presence of other people. The sights and sounds of others can convey tons of desire to continue pursuing your ultimate vision. You need two kinds of people to help you.

First, you need authorities, such as coaches, trainers, professionals and even training partners of higher rank. Remember your corner? These people can be a very good source of encouragement and motivation for you. People of authority have a way of making the issue of continuing or quitting a nonissue. Hearing from them and being around them may remind you that quitting never was and never will be an option for you. They have a way of generating an aura of persistence that is quite contagious. Catch it from them and make it your own. If you truly look up to these people, let them inspire you to keep at it.

You also need peers of positive influence. Any difficult journey is made easier with a little help and support from friends. Draw strength and encouragement from the people you know will help you stay on course; keep on track and in the fight.

A note of warning: If you find yourself avoiding these kinds of people, it may be because your vision and your resolve are waning. The idea of quitting may already be taking root in the back of your mind, so your authorities and comrades make you feel more uncomfortable. If that is the case, refuse and reject it outright. It is an indication that you need their encouragement and motivation all the more to keep your vision clear and your desire strong.

MAKE YOUR VISION REAL THROUGH PERSISTENCE

The end result of visualization techniques is the development of persistence, and that is what will turn your future vision into current reality.

Only persistence has the power to overcome all the strengths of an opponent and all of your weaknesses. It is the most necessary part in the solution to most problems. Only persistence leads to success. Only through persistence will any of the other techniques and methods listed in this book work at all. You can have the best information, the best plans and the best of intentions, but without persistence, it won't amount to much. That's because it doesn't matter what you do once or twice, every now and then, occasionally or for a while. It only matters what you do persistently to the very end.

Persistence is at the core of determining ultimate success or failure in many ventures.

The very title of this book is an expression of the characteristic of persistence. It absolutely demands persistence on your part to recover as fully as possible from an injury. Are you up to it? Do you have the long-range fire in the belly to see it through? If not, you are in serious jeopardy of falling short of your finest goals, and you may face ultimate failure for one reason and one reason only: You quit.

Persistence is the opposite of quitting. Consider losing a fight. Would you rather lose because you are beaten fair and square or because you quit? Exactly. The person who does not persist quits. But you are not that kind of person. You are not a quitter, and the great characteristic of persistence is going to stand you in good stead in all areas of life, not just in your martial arts career and injury recovery.

So decide what you want, what you can believe in and what you look forward to. Let the power of your mind develop and impassion the desire that will drive you to persistence and ultimately to optimized health and wellness. Get yourself fired up about the good things that are going to happen to you. Dwell on them. Emotionalize them in your mind and let that zeal program your subconscious mind into action. Surround yourself with positive people and things, and let your senses pick up on those positives energies and transfer them to your subconscious. This all builds your capacity for persistence and puts the grandest of visions within your reach.

**From Your Corner:
Joe Lewis**

Ask martial artists why they train, and they may say, "Well, I haven't thought about that lately." I'll bet they never thought about it!

When you start a workout, raise your self-consciousness and ask, "Why am I working out today?" Halfway through the workout, ask yourself that again.

Start asking yourself, "Why?" Why are you still training? Why did you do that workout?

Don't ask "what" you are going to do, but why you are going to do it. It's like dieting. Don't talk about what you are going to do, and what you are going to eat. Instead, ask yourself "why." Why do I eat? You will find that the diet becomes much easier.

It's that way with training. Settle the issues of "why," and you'll find the motivation and inspiration to stay with it.

**From Your Corner:
Danny Dring**

In my travels through the waiting rooms of many medical professionals, I've seen a lot of people with lesser injuries than my own who never recovered, never regained an athletic lifestyle, never even got off a walker. They just didn't want it badly enough. You've got to passionately want to get better. You've got to demand it of yourself. Quitting is easy; persistence is hard, but it's worth it.

CHAPTER ELEVEN
WHEN YOU CAN'T COME BACH

You've been waiting for that opening and there it is. Crack! You feel the satisfying thud of your fist against his chin, right on the button. Down he goes, down and out. The Ref steps in, calls him out, and the crowd goes wild. He holds up your hand, and you are announced the winner. You are having a great time and a part of you wishes it could go on forever, but you are tired and battered, your breathing is still labored and stiffness is setting in as soon as you begin to cool down. You know it's time to take off your gear, cut off the tape, hang up your gloves and walk away.

It's a fact of life that sooner or later, one way or another, you will no longer be able to come back. It happens to everyone. For some, there is the injury that is severe enough to be dubbed "career ending." For some, there is the catastrophic event in life such as an automobile accident or devastating illness. For some, there is the call of duty, which results in the martial career being put on hold, sometimes indefinitely. For some, there is the injury incurred in the line of duty, as an law-enforcement officer on the street or as a soldier on the field of battle. For all, there is the unceasing march of time. Years will pass, and so will our athleticism.

So what do you do when you can't come back but want to stay in the fight? Here is the short answer: Accept it and move on. However, there is a lot more to it than just that pithy cliché. Let's take a closer look at just what is involved.

As a martial athlete, you are probably less likely to quit when you don't have to and more likely to keep trying when you can't. You may tend to be in denial about your diminishing athleticism, but it will eventually sink in. You will eventually face reality, and you will know when the "comeback" is simply no longer an option.

One of the dangers here is the temptation to prove that you've still got it. Buying a giant motorcycle, picking a fight, doubling up on workouts and any other number of activities may seem like handy testing grounds to show the world that you are still the world's most dangerous warrior, but they aren't. Neither is spending all your time re-counting your old days of glory a good option. It's true that no one can take away your accomplishments, but it is equally true that they are stuck in the past. Don't be stuck there with them.

At the end of the day, reality hasn't changed and you are still in need of a way to move forward. That's the thing: You can't be looking back or living in the past while moving forward at the same time. You have to choose one or the other. So remember two very important principles:

• to accept change is not the same as accepting defeat
• when you can't come back, you can still go forward

You CAN move on, and you CAN weather the changes of life. Remember that, unlike many other athletic endeavors, there is a place for you in martial arts for as long as you live.

DETERMINE TO BE A MARTIAL ATHLETE FOR LIFE

One thing that sets martial arts apart from many other athletic endeavors is that you can pursue it for life. The world of martial arts is filled with people in their 70s, 80s and beyond that are still active, still training and still reaping the benefits of the martial arts life. Your martial arts career will certainly go through some changes, but you can be involved in martial arts in some capacity for as long as you can move.

Make the determination in your heart and mind that the world of martial arts is part of who you are and not just something that you do. This can help fix a deep-seated attitude of athleticism in your psyche that will go a long way in keeping you active in both mind and body.

Remember, years from now you won't be saying to people, "I used to do martial arts." Instead, you will be telling them, "I am a martial artist." See the difference?

From Your Corner:
Joe Lewis

I've been to the top, and I know what it's like from age 15 to 20, 20 to 30, to 40, 50, all the way up to age 65. And you know what I've discovered?

There is a difference between what your body needs, what's really important to you as a human being, and "ego goals."

Many martial artists start out wanting to achieve titles, win an important position, become head instructor, or to be famous, appreciated, recognized and win awards. These are ego-driven goals. But when you get older, you find out all that is nonsense.

Instead of all that, try to think about being potential-oriented. In other words, what development and fulfillment of potential can you strive for?

Not everybody has the potential to be a black belt, to win a championship, to be a great martial artist and be appreciated as such, but everybody can strive to maximize their potential.

Life is about growing, and so you say to yourself, how can I better contribute to the core processes of who I am? In terms of your mind, spirit, body, emotions, self-worth and your sense of "self," how can you actualize your fullest potential?

Focus in that direction. Look at yourself as a human being and have a strong "self" concept. The way to do that, to elevate your consciousness, is to keep your brain working and to keep striving all the time to learn something new.

If you go from that perspective, it is easier to create a stronger, more realistic vision of where you want to be, and then set your goals. You'll stay active longer, and you'll have more fun in the martial arts!

REDEFINE YOUR GOALS (AGAIN)

The age old question, "Who am I?" too often goes unanswered in today's busy world. But when you are no longer certain as to what you can DO, you can still know who you ARE.

Is there more to you than your physical prowess? When your usual outlets of self-expression are taken from you, is there anything else? When your career as a fighter is gone, is there anything left?

Of course there is. Here are some possibilities:

- **Keep learning:** There will always be new things to learn and discover. The very act of learning, thinking and growing in a mental capacity can have the effect of slowing the aging processes in the mind. There is even research that indicates an active, learning mind literally wards off decline not only in mental capacity, but even slows the deterioration of the brain and its functions that come with aging. For a martial artist, loss of interest can be a sure sign of getting "old." Fight it, keep your interest in life and keep learning.

- **Focus on technique:** You have probably been taught from your very first martial arts class the importance of skill and good technique. You were probably told, and rightly so, that in a contest between strength and skill, all else being equal, the odds were in favor of skill. What makes the "greats" in martial arts so great? Is it their amazing strength and stamina, or is it the amazing skill and technique developed over the years by which they can have their way with younger, bigger and stronger opponents? As an athlete faced with the certainty that strength will eventually decline, you understand that your technical ability becomes of greater importance with each passing year. Determine to be "great," to be skilled, and to be a martial technician.

- **Change your game:** When hard charging, full contact martial arts is no longer an option for you, perhaps you can find another discipline to your liking. Consider cross-training in a variety of styles. Perhaps you will enjoy a style that focuses on very precise and technical points such as weapons or kata. Perhaps you are a professional and you just need to throttle back and "retire" some of your intensity by participating as a coach or training partner.

- **Focus on alternative activities:** In the world of martial arts, there are many alternative activities besides fighting. Consider the need in schools for coaching, training and teaching. Consider specializing your ability to educate others in some niche such as law enforcement, children's martial arts or self-defense. Consider also being involved in competition by judging, refereeing or working the corner. There are also needs for knowledgeable people for announcing, critiquing, reporting and writing. It may be that you can redirect your martial career in one or more of these areas.

- **Focus on the business side:** There are a lot of business opportunities in the world of martial arts. Consider working at or starting a school or working the business side of a school while someone else does the teaching. There is a need for someone to effectively recruit students, find sponsors and write grants. You may want to start your own seminars and sell your own products.
- **Give back:** It can be very fulfilling to give back to the sport and the community that has given much to you. Avenues include doing volunteer teaching at a local martial arts school, motivational speaking, teaching at an afterschool program or instructing disadvantaged youth.

Aside from the obvious payoffs of all these avenues for continued involvement in the martial lifestyle, there are some other important benefits. For example, when you are involved in coaching and training, you are forced to keep your own abilities up to par. You have to be able to do it in order to teach it. That will help keep you active and goal-oriented. As an instructor, you will also have to constantly repeat your most important beliefs and stay true to them. Having students is an excellent way to make sure you are always a student yourself.

Investing in others always ends up being a great investment in yourself. Everybody wins. When you start to focus outward on others instead of dwelling on your own issues and problems, you find that it gives you a new and stronger definition of yourself and sense of purpose. You will thus begin to see your own troubles as less significant and your opportunities as greater.

The great thing about life is that you get to start fresh every day. So in the spirit of leaving the past in the past, begin to focus on your future and on the person you would like to become. If you can't be the heavyweight champion of the world, then who do you want to be?

If you've been diligent in your work on your positive mental attitude and vision, you will know that you still live in a world of great possibilities, regardless of declining athleticism. You'll believe that although the body may decline, you still have a lot of opportunities for involvement and growth as a martial athlete. Look around in your world for new paths. Get creative, decide who you want to be and what you want to do, and go for it.

It is true that a person's physical athleticism inevitably declines, but the person who has fought for optimal athleticism regardless of circumstances can rest assured that their reduced degree of athleticism will still far outstrip that of many average people.

So remember that a physically declining martial athlete is still a martial athlete, and that growth and mastery will always remain worthy goals for life.

Hopefully, that with experience comes wisdom, not only in fighting, but in all areas of life. It is also hoped that dealing with injury and decline will simply bring an inner strength that not only is rare but defies explanation. There is a difference between just existing and truly living. Only by the cumulative effect of life experiences can anyone expect to know what a day of life is really worth, and to make the most of each one. Now that's staying in the fight.

Bruce Lee to me: "Joe, I'm a student-master, you know why? Because I am a master, but I'm always learning; I am a student. So realistically, I am a student-master."

That's it: sometimes an instructor, always a student. Sometimes an expert, always a student.

Think that way, and it will keep your brain young. If your brain is young, the body and everything else will be young. But if you don't keep the brain young, it ain't going to last.

CHAPTER TWELVE
CELEBRATE

You are elated! The fight is over and the "W" is in the bag. Standing straight and tall before the judges, you hear your name called and step forward. Amid the applause of the crowd you bow, accept your trophy and raise it high into the air.

Congratulations, you've made an excellent comeback! You've worked hard physically and mentally toward regaining the greatest level of martial athleticism you can. Perhaps you feel that you are near or back to where you were pre-injury. Perhaps you even are ready to reset the goals and dreams you had for yourself before injury forced you to put them on the back burner.

As you reach the completion of your major goals, you will realize that they were in reality short- or medium-term goals, and now you have the wonderful privilege of setting more long-term goals for yourself and your martial career.

Here are a few things to take into consideration as you embrace your newfound future:

- Remember the lessons you learned during the recovery process. You have probably gleaned very valuable information, experience and life skills from them. Perhaps you have also settled some inner issues. If that is the case for you, then hold onto the good that has come out of your injury. If it is truly adversity that tempers the steel, then be tempered. On a more practical note, remember that you did suffer an injury and that you may not be as completely healed as you feel. Many injuries leave permanent changes in physiology, and no amount of recovery will completely erase all evidence of injury. That's what a scar is all about.

- Who has helped you in your time of need? Who has played a part in the progress that you are enjoying? They should be included in your celebration. Let your whole support system know that you are improving and making progress. You never know how much good can be done and encouragement given just by simply saying "thank you" and including others in your time of celebration.

- Revel in your progress, and enjoy your success. Take time to roll it around in your heart and mind; it is good for you. Not only is it fun to mark your progress, but it will also serve to strengthen your resolve to continue and your ability to focus and keep a positive mental attitude. A healthy dose of inner and outer celebration is good for the spirit of gratitude and persistence that are needed for continued progress, which will in turn provide more reasons to celebrate.

- Last, remember that you were probably injured while you were healthy. So if the healthy you can be injured so can the recovered you. Add an extra layer of protection to the recovered area any way you can. A brace or a wrap, an extra soak in the hot tub, a few extra minutes to warm up or an extra round of icing after workout may help the recovered area grow even stronger.

The purpose of this book is not only to help you recover from an injury, but to assist you in your quest to be a true champion in the process. More than merely the winner of a contest, a champion is one who lives a life of character, integrity and honor.

Your journey through injury and recovery has built character by instilling a passionate desire for worthwhile goals, a strong work ethic, determination and self-discipline. It has developed in you integrity, which is character displayed over time. You have shown that integrity by staying in the fight against injury and seeing it to its end. Finally, your battle against adversity has distinguished you with honor. You have shown great heart to have made it this far, survived testing, won victories, regained what was lost or faced permanent injury with grace and dignity.

Good job, well done, you are still in the fight!

From Your Corner: Robson Moura, Seven-time World BJJ champ

When I was training in Brazil, this guy went for an armbar. My elbow was hyperextended and my bicep was injured. I couldn't work out, couldn't train—couldn't even do push-ups.

The doctor said I had to take a long break from hard training, and that made me upset for sure, but I found out I could do some light exercises and so I did them every single day. I used ice and did what the doctor said. I also did a lot of stretching and still taught my class every day.

One of the good things that happened was that this let many smaller injuries recover at the same time. Another very important thing at that time was how my wife helped me to do other things to take my mind off my injury. We played golf and did some other things that I didn't have time to do before since I was so focused on my training. It was not too bad since I could keep busy, and the time seemed to go by quickly.

When the doctor let me train again my bicep was not very strong and it took a long time to recover all the way. I still have to warm up pretty good before I train or do my workout, and I keep a close watch on my bicep.

Notice

Champion Robson Moura did much of what is presented in this book. He:

- followed his doctor's directions concerning healing and rehabilitation.
- trained around his injury by doing what exercises he could every day.
- focused on developing greater flexibility in his lower body while his arm healed.
- kept a positive mental attitude by understanding that during downtime, lesser injuries would also have time to heal.
- proactively continued to teach and attend his classes.
- stayed busy with other things in life and made time for other priorities, such as spending more time with his wife.
- engaged in posthab after doctor's release by training the recovering area gently.
- avoided re-injury by understanding that it would take a long time to fully recover.
- continues to avoid re-injury by taking a little extra time to warm up the recovered area, as the effects of injury linger on.

APPENDIX A
ATHLETIC EXERCISES

The stretches and exercises in this section are listed as examples and are included as some of the exercises I have personally used to overcome various injuries. The following movements are not a complete representation of everything I did for recovery, but they are listed because they are good fundamental exercises that I still include in my daily routine to maintain my health and fitness.

You'll notice postural alignment is demonstrated first because all the exercises and stretches should first begin with good posture. Thus, take care to maintain postural alignment while performing any exercise or stretch.

From there, I'll go to neck warm-up exercises, then work my way down my body before progressing to floor exercises. I've also included a couple of exercises for the common complaint of shin splints. Last, because shoulder injuries are common concerns for martial artists and athletes of all styles, I've included a handful of exercises for shoulders. In the end, all these exercises and stretches continue to help keep me in the fight.

Before you perform any of the following stretches or exercises, please consult with the members of your team to be absolutely certain you are physically ready to perform the exercises. Your professionals may also want to recommend variations of the exercises because of individual concerns you may have with your particular condition.

As you progress with your exercises, for example, you may want to add weight gradually to increase your strength. After my shoulder surgery, I began with one-pound weights and progressed upward from there to a heavier weight. I recommend that you also start with a light weight and only move up in weight when you can perform the exercise with perfect form for 10 to 15 repetitions. Remember these exercises are for posthab or, if you are recovered, pre-workout, so your repetition format may be a little higher. During all the exercises and stretches, remember to breathe.

When stretching, be careful not to strain yourself. A gentle, constant pull that you can relax into will yield results while jerking or straining can cause you to injure yourself. Finally, I recommend you hold all of your stretches for 10 to 30 seconds. If you find you are really tight in a particular muscle group that is being stretched, then you may want to hold the stretch for up to two minutes. Again, remember to breathe and come out of the stretches slowly while maintaining good posture.

Enjoy!

—Danny Dring

Postural Alignment

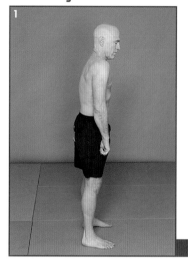 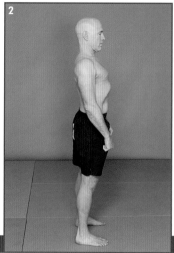

1: Poor Posture: The back is arched and the shoulders are slumped forward.

2: Good Posture: The back is straight and the shoulders are pulled back so the chest is high.

Neck Stretch No. 1

1: Start with the head up and look straight ahead.

2: Tilt the head down and look at the ground.

3: Return the head to the original head-up position, looking straight ahead.

4: Turn your head to the left as far as possible. Look straight in that direction.

5: Come back to center, looking straight ahead. Turn your head to the opposite side.

Neck Stretch No. 2

1: Extend your left arm out straight.

2: Reach it up and over your head.

3: Pull your ear to your shoulder gently, then repeat this stretch on the other side. Note: Keep your shoulders down and relaxed during this stretch.

Neck Stretch No. 3

1: Turn your head to the right and extend the right arm to that side.

2: Reach your right arm over your head and palm the back of your head.

3: Gently pull your head down and feel the stretch in the back of the neck. Repeat this stretch on the other side.

Neck Stretch No. 4

  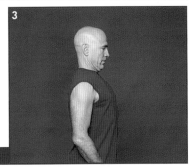

1: Stand with good posture with your head pushed back. Your forehead and chin should be in line.

2: Jut your head forward.

3: Return to your starting position. Repeat this action four to six times.

Neck Exercise No. 1

1: Place both hands on your forehead. Push your head back while pushing forward with your head, thus forming an isometric resistance, which builds strength through tension.

Neck Exercise No. 2

1: Repeat the process in No. 5, but this time place your hands behind your head and pull forward while pushing back with you head.

Neck Exercise No. 3

1-2: Do the same isometric exercise in No. 5 and No. 6, but this time push the sides of the head.

Shoulder Warm-Up Exercise No. 1

1: With your arms fully extended in front of you, make two fists. Stick out your thumbs so they touch each other.

2-3: Spread your arms out until they are fully extended.

Note: Remember to keep tension between the shoulder blades when at full extension.

4: Return to your starting position and repeat it on the opposite side. Do 10 reps on each side.

Shoulder Warm-Up Exercise No. 2

1: Repeat the process at an angle.

2: Extend your arms at an angle. Keep tension between your shoulders, too.

3: Repeat the exercise on the opposite side. Do 10 reps on each side.

Shoulder Warm-Up Exercise No. 3

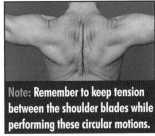

Note: Remember to keep tension between the shoulder blades while performing these circular motions.

1: Extend your arms to the side as if pushing apart two people. Make small circles with your arms both in a forward and backward direction.

Shoulder Warm-Up Exercise No. 4

1: Start in your standing position with good posture. Your hands hang at your sides. Turn the right palm so it faces away from your body.

2: Keeping the palm to the outside, move your arm up in front of the body, beginning a circular motion.

3: Continue raising your arm until it is straight up. It's OK to extend your shoulder during this stretch because you can really exaggerate the reach of this circle.

4: Keep moving your arm with the palm facing outward behind you.

5-6: The arm has made a complete circle but will continue up until it is straight in front of you parallel to the floor.

7: Reach under the outstretched arm with the opposite arm and pull the outstretched arm across your chest. Hold the stretch for 10 to 30 seconds before releasing. Repeat this movement on the opposite side.

Shoulder Warm-Up Exercise No. 5

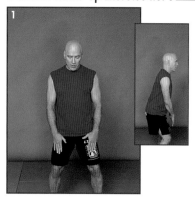

1: Stand with your knees bent and back straight. Your arms hang down straight in front of you, as if you are holding an imaginary bar.

2: Raise your elbows level with your shoulders and maintain shoulder tension between your shoulder blades. Note: Anytime you lift your chest, you want to contract your shoulders.

3: With your elbows level to your shoulders, rotate your fists up toward the ceiling.

4: Press your arms up until they are fully extended overhead.

5: Bring your arms down until your elbows are level with your shoulders.

6: Rotate your hands toward the ground.

7: Lower your arms to the starting position.

Shoulder Wall Stretch

1: Stand about four to six inches away from a wall. Extend your arm straight up the wall with the palm of your hand resting on the wall.

2-3: Work your arm gradually in a circle behind you by opening your fingers and closing them to inch your arm backward.

4-5: Continue this motion of inching your arm slowly backward. Take your time.

6: Continue until your arm is at your side and hold the stretch for 10 to 30 seconds. When done, you can just release the stretch by moving away from the wall. Repeat on the other arm. Note: For people with serious flexibility issues, I recommend you hold the stretch for upwards of two minutes because it takes longer for the muscle to relax.

Rolling Out the Hips

1: Stand with good posture and your feet shoulder-width apart.

2-4: Push your hips to each side in a circular motion.

5-8: For a variation, try doing the exercise with one leg extended at an angle in front of you. Repeat on the opposite side.

Pushing the Hips to the Front and Back

1: Stand with good posture with your feet shoulder-width apart and hands on your hips.

2: Push your hips back until you feel your weight over your heels. Remember to keep your knees straight.

3: Then push your hips as far forward as possible until you feel your weight over the balls of your feet.

Hip-Flexor Stretch Using a Bench

1: Extend your leg behind you, placing the ball of your foot on a chair or bench. Maintain good posture while in this position.

2: Lean back while keeping your leg straight and your chest lifted. This intensifies the stretch in your hip-flexor. Repeat this stretch on the opposite side.

More Hip Work With a Bench

1: Standing next to a bench or chair, raise your leg to your side and place it so your foot is parallel to the ground.

2: Keep your back in line with your leg and lean toward the foot on the bench.

3: Then lean away from the foot on the bench while still keeping your back in line with your leg. Repeat this stretch on the opposite leg.

4-5: Another exercise you can do on the bench is a variation of Pushing the Hips to the Front and Back. This time you keep one foot on the bench. Repeat the stretch on the opposite leg.

Hamstring Stretch

1: While standing with good posture, place one leg on a bench or chair with your toes pointed toward the ceiling.

2: Begin pushing your hips back stretching your chest forward. When stretching this way, keep your back straight because it maximizes the stretch in your hamstring and reduces the chance of injury.

3: Reach for your foot to intensify the stretch. Remember to keep your chest lifted. Hold for 10 to 30 seconds.

4-5: Keeping your chest lifted, slowly return to upright position. Make sure to repeat the stretch on the opposite leg. Note: If you find it difficult to return to the original position, use your hands to walk back up the leg to an upright position.

Hamstring Stretch and Strengthener

1: Balance on one leg while holding your other leg parallel to the ground behind you.

2: Keeping your supporting leg straight, stretch forward with the chest lifted while pushing your hips back.

3: Reach down and touch the ground while keeping the supporting leg straight.

4: Return to an upright position by focusing on the contraction of the standing leg's hamstring.

5: Maintain your balance and return to your upright position. Repeat on the opposite side.

Quadriceps Stretch No. 1

1: Standing with good posture, bring your foot up to your buttocks and grab that foot or shin with your same-side hand.

2: Pull your leg back until you feel the stretch in your quad. Repeat this stretch on the opposite side.

3: If your balance isn't steady, use a chair or bench for balance so you can focus on the stretch.

Quadriceps Stretch No. 2

1: If you're quite flexible already and have good balance, then you can do the archer's pose from yoga. Do the regular quadriceps stretch. When you pull your leg back, extend the opposite arm in front of you and lean forward at the waist. Also extend the foot you are holding to the ceiling.

2: If your balance isn't steady, use a chair or bench for balance so you can focus on the stretch.

Round-Kick Stretch

1: While using a bench for balance, pick up your leg as if performing a round kick. Grab your shin fairly close to your knee.

2: Push your hips forward while pulling your leg back until you feel the stretch in your hip flexor and quadriceps.

3: Maintaining this posture, pull your knee as high as possible. You may feel the stretch in your groin and supporting leg. Relax into the stretch.

Calf Stretch No. 1

1: Stand with good posture and your legs shoulder-width apart. Reach one leg back behind you, extending the ball of your foot to the ground.

2: Push your heel to the ground while maintaining an upright posture. Feel the stretch in the calf.

3: A variation of this stretch is to put your hands on the wall and push your heel back on ground.

113

Calf Stretch No. 2

1: Place the ball of the foot on a sturdy object. Here, I am using a dumbbell.

2: Begin pushing the hips back while keeping the chest lifted and the back straight to lean forward. Hold the stretch for 10 to 30 seconds before slowly releasing the position.

Butterfly Stretch

1: Sit with your back straight and your legs bent so that the bottoms of your feet are touching.

2: Raise your knees as close together as you can.

3: Lower your knees as far as possible.

4: Lean forward with your chest lifted and back straight. Use your arms to walk yourself out as far as possible. Note: Throughout this entire stretch you should have a straight back and lifted chest.

Danny Dring and Johnny D. Taylor

Straddle Stretch No. 1 and No. 2

1: Sit on the ground with your legs comfortably spread apart. Your posture should still be erect.

2: Stretching forward with your chest lifted, lean to one side.

3: Return to your original position, then stretch to the other side.

4: Return to your original position and stretch to the center.

5: Looking to one side, put a hand on either side of that side's leg. Push yourself toward the foot you are looking at. This will increase your stretch.

6-8: Your straddle is now farther apart so you need to stretch to the left, right and center again. Keep repeating these four steps until you reach your maximum straddle.

9: Eventually, you will be able to achieve a fully stretched position.

115

Back Stretch No. 1

1: Sit on the floor with both legs extended straight out in front of you. Sit with good upright posture.

2: Reach forward with extended arms. Stretch forward with your chest lifted and back relatively straight.

3: Grab your feet and maintain the stretch for 10 to 30 seconds before gently returning to the beginning position.

4: To intensify this stretch, sit with your back to a wall and your legs stretched out in front of you. Use your hands to gently push your body forward, thus intensifying the stretch.

Back Stretch No. 2

1: Sit with both legs extended straight out in front of you.

2: Pull one leg toward your body so that the bottom of your foot rests against the inside thigh of the outstretched leg.

3: Reach out with both hands and stretch with the chest lifted to the shin or foot, if possible, of the leg that is stretched straight.

4: Gently pull yourself into the stretch and hold for 10 to 30 seconds before returning to the upright position.

Back Stretch No. 3

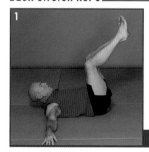  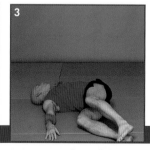

1: Lay on your back with your arms stretched out straight level with your elbows in a "T" position. Hold your legs up in the air. Keep your knees bent.

2: Lower your legs to one side with control while looking to the other side and exhaling.

3: Lower your legs all the way to the floor. Relax into the stretch and hold it for 10 to 30 seconds. Using your abs, slowly raise your legs. Repeat the stretch on the other side.

Back Stretch No. 4

1: Lay on your back with your arms stretched out straight level with your elbows in a "T" position. Hold your legs up in the air. Keep your knees bent.

2: With control, place the balls of your feet on the ground close to your buttocks.

3: Drive your hips into the air, bridging up as high as possible.

4: Intensify this stretch by grabbing your ankles. When you release the stretch, come down with control by lowering your back one vertebra at a time.

Shin-Splint Exercise No. 1

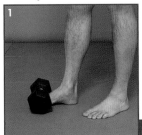 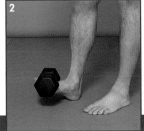 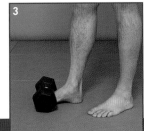

1: Place your foot under a light dumbbell so that your toes can lift up and hold the bar from underneath.

2: Lift and hold the dumbbell with your foot for 10 seconds.

3: Lower the bell with control to the ground. Repeat for 10 reps, then switch to the other side.

Shin-Splint Exercise No. 2

1: Stand on one foot and extend the other foot. Hold the extended foot just off of the ground.

2-4: Now pretend that your big toe is a pen and trace the letters of the alphabet in the air. This will move your ankle through a complete range of motion. It will also serve to strengthen your ankle and help alleviate your shin splints.

Shoulder Exercise With Weights No. 1

1: Lay on your side with your top leg bent so that that foot is flat on the floor. Your weighted arm is bent at a 90-degree angle with the dumbbell on the floor.

2: Keeping the bent-arm elbow in place on your body, rotate your arm to the ceiling.

3: Extend your arm straight into the air.

4: Lower your arm until the elbow touches your body again.

5: Rotate your arm until the dumbbell returns to the floor.

Shoulder Exercise With Weights No. 2

1: With weight plates in your hands, stand with your knees bent and back straight. Your arms hang straight down in front of you. Note: You can also do this exercise with dumbbells.

2: Raise your elbows level with your shoulders.

3: With your elbows level to your shoulders, rotate your hands up toward the ceiling.

4: Press your arms up until they fully extended overhead.

5: Lower your arms until your elbows are level with your shoulders.

6: Rotate your hands so the weights are now toward the ground.

7: Lower your arms to the starting position. Note: This is the same as the exercise that was performed on page 108 without weight. This exercise just adds more resistance building strength.

Shoulder Exercise With Weights No. 3

1: Hold a pair of dumbbells at your side with good posture.

2: Raise the dumbbells up in front of you with your arms parallel to the floor. Your shoulders should remain level.

3: Turn the dumbbells slowly inward as if pouring water out of a glass.

4: Return the dumbbells to an upright position while keeping your arms parallel to the floor.

5: Lower your arms to the starting position.

Shoulder Exercise With Weights No. 4

1: Hold a pair of dumbbells at your side with good posture. Keep them light, between five and 15 pounds.

2-3: Raise your arms up at a 45-degree angle from your body.

4: Turn the dumbbells slowly inward as if pouring water from a glass.

5-6: Return the dumbbells to an upright position while keeping your arms parallel to the floor.

Shoulder Exercise With Weights No.5

1: Hold a pair of dumbbells at your side with good posture. Keep them light, between five and 15 pounds.

2: This time, raise your arms straight to the side until they are parallel to the floor in a "T" position.

3: Turn the dumbbells slowly inward to once again imitate the action of pouring water from a glass.

4: Return the dumbbells to an upright position.

5: Slowly lower your arms to the starting position.

Coach John Davies Shoulder Exercise With a Band and Tennis Ball No. 1

1: Take a tennis ball and exercise band.

2: Wrap the tennis ball in one end of the exercise band and step on the other end of the band with the foot opposite to the hand holding the tennis ball.

3: Perform a lateral raise by lifting the arm to your side until it is parallel to the ground.

4: For added resistance, step on the band with both feet.

5: Perform the lateral raise again. Remember to switch sides.

121

Coach John Davies Shoulder Exercise With a Band and Tennis Ball No. 2

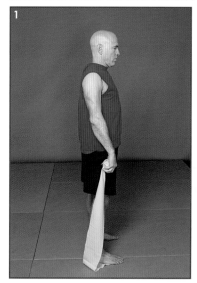

1: Stand on one end of the band with the tennis ball wrapped in the band held in your same-side hand.

2: Raise your elbow so it is level with your shoulder.

3: With your elbow level with your shoulder, rotate your arm up toward the ceiling.

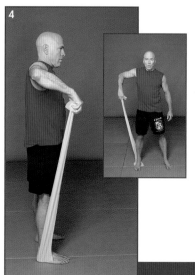

4: Rotate your arm back toward the ground while maintaining your elbow at shoulder level.

5: Return to the starting position and switch sides.

APPENDIX B
LIST OF CONTRIBUTORS

John Davies is the founder of Renegade Training International, Coach John Davies is a world renown trainer in human performance and functional training. A much sought after consultant for many professional sports teams and dozens of NCAA institutions, he is known by many for his work with soccer luminary Diego Maradona. In addition to his duties with a worldwide consulting practice, Davies is a proud contributor for USP Labs as a writer within the exercise, strength and conditioning fields. He is the author of nine books including *Renegade Training for Football*, *Xtreme Sports Training* and *The Mark of R Part II: The Rebirth of Honor*. To learn more about John Davies, visit www.renegadetraining.com.

Mark Graden is the former director of martial arts curriculum for the National Association of Professional Martial Artists. In that role, he coordinated the curriculum content of every monthly NAPMA Professional Package and bimonthly NAPMA Squared Package. Graden also prepared the monthly NAPMA Sounds of Success CD and NAPMA Innovations DVD. He also worked closely with many leading martial arts professionals and instructors to prepare and produce NAPMA's selection of comprehensive curriculums and programs. Graden has been a martial arts video producer for almost 20 years—10 years with NAPMA.

Graden is a fifth-degree black belt under Joe Lewis, having trained for more than 30 years, and a world-class WAKO Kickboxing fighter. He was named the 2005 and 2006 Pound-for-Pound Fighter of the Year by the board of directors of Joe Lewis Fighting Systems. Graden is also the master instructor at World Champion Jim Graden's Karate in Seminole, Florida.

David S. Klein, M.D. is the founder of the Pain Center of Orlando, Inc. He specializes in the diagnosis and treatment of pain, pain-related problems and hormonal dysfunction. Trained at the Universities of Maryland and North Carolina and Duke University, he holds six medical-board certifications and has over 24 years experience in pain medicine.

A decorated Gulf War veteran, Dr. Klein served seven years as a Navy physician and five years as an Air Force flight surgeon. In his current practice, he treats many martial artists and the injuries typically sustained in a martial arts lifestyle.

He also is a prolific writer and speaker, having made contributions to medical journals and martial arts publications as well as having appeared at martial arts events. To learn more about Dr. Klein visit www.suffernomore.com or his blog at paindoctor. typepad.com/martial_arts_injuries.

Joe Lewis: Grandmaster Joe Lewis is a 10th-degree black belt who was voted Greatest Karate Fighter of All Time by *Black Belt* and twice voted to *Black Belt*'s Hall of Fame as the 1975 Fighter of the Year and 1986 Co-Instructor of the Year. He has won more titles and set more records in his career than anyone yet in the history of sport karate. Lewis won U.S. National Karate Championships four times between the years 1966 and 1971. He also won 3 consecutive grand championship titles at the International Karate Championships in between 1969 and 1971. Lewis won the world heavyweight karate championship in 1968, which combined with his kickboxing title meant that Lewis was the first of only two people to hold world titles in two different fighting sports. On September 14, 1974, he introduced kickboxing on ABC's Wide World of Entertainment and is recognized as the father of American kickboxing. Founder of the Joe Lewis Fighting Systems, he currently teaches dozens of seminars around the world each year in addition to hosting an annual research conference for the members of his organization. To learn more about Joe Lewis, visit www.joelewisfightingsystems.com.

Robson Moura is a seven-time world champion in Brazilian *jiu-jitsu*. He is the founder and head instructor of Robson Moura Academy. To learn more about Robson Moura, visit robsonmoura.com.

Bill Wallace began studying karate in 1967 after a leg injury prevented him from practicing judo, his first martial art. Though he was unable to kick with his right leg, he excelled in karate and competed in tournaments across the country, capturing virtually every major title on the tournament circuit. To his credit, Wallace defended his title as the Professional Karate Association's middleweight champion a total of 23 times. He has won multiple U.S. championships, the U.S. Karate Association Grand National and the Top 10 Nationals. Wallace has been inducted twice into *Black Belt*'s Hall of Fame as the 1977 Competitor of the Year and the 1978 Man of the Year, thus making him a bonafide martial arts legend. He teaches seminars all over the world and remains one of the industry's most respected personalities. To learn more about Bill Wallace, visit www.superfoot.com.

Mark Young is sports therapist, licensed massage therapist and certified strength-and-conditioning specialist in Little Rock, Arkansas. To learn more about Mark Young, visit life-letics.com.

FIGHTSHEETS

The following worksheets are designed to help you build your own customized plan for achieving your optimal health and athleticism. Work through them carefully as you make your way through the book, putting thought and study into each entry. It is important that you complete the entire book and all the accompanying Fightsheets, because every subject covered has a direct bearing on the degree and speed of your recovery. To download the Fightsheets, go to www.blackbeltmag.com/fightsheets.

Fightsheet 1

The Fight of Your Life

- What do you hope to accomplish through the processes outlined in this book?

- What injuries are you dealing with?

- Whom do you know that has suffered athletic injury?

- Who else has sustained injury or adversity similar to your own?

- Who has successfully recovered from your type of injury?

Your objective is to achieve "optimal health and wellness." Describe what that will be like.

Commit yourself to the pursuit of this worthy goal by signing the statement below. Make this PROMISE TO YOURSELF, and post a copy of it where you will see it often.

I am a fighter and I am going to achieve optimal health and wellness to the best of my ability.

I WILL: Take responsibility for my health, healing and wellness.

I WILL: Carry out my customized, comprehensive plan as laid out in my Fightsheets.

Signature: _____ Date: _____

Fightsheet 2

The Six Dimensions of Athletic Health

How has your injury affected your body as a whole?

STRENGTH:

- How has injury affected your physical strength specifically?

- What strengthening exercises are you currently able to perform as you recover? (Note: Consult your medical professional before starting an exercise regimen.)

CARDIO:

- How has injury affected your cardio?

- What cardio exercises are you able to do as you recover?

- What specific equipment such as a jump rope, heavy bag, rowing machine and treadmill can you use to increase your cardio?

FLEXIBILITY:

- How has injury affected your range of motion?

- What areas of your body can you currently work on to increase flexibility?

- What stretching routines can you do for these areas?

NUTRITION:

Determine what you need to do to achieve balanced and complete nutrition in the following categories.

Protein: _____

Carbohydrates: _____

Fats: _____

Vitamins: _____

Minerals: _____

Other supplements such as botanicals: _____

(See the list of supplements on page 70 for some recommendations.)
   • Where will you get these nutritional supplements?

HYDRATION:

   • How much water do you need as you recover, based on your current level of physical activity?

   • What is going to be your primary source of water? (bottled, filtered, tap, etc.)

   • Are you currently displaying any signs of dehydration such as dry mouth, chapped lips, dark urine or dry skin?

   • Do any of your medications act as a diuretic to reduce the amount of water in your tissues? If so, find out what your doctor suggests to counteract any adverse affects in overall hydration.

REST:

- In light of your current health and wellness, how much rest do you need on a daily basis?

- How much are you currently getting?

- What specifically do you need to do in order to bring your resting time in line with your health and wellness needs?

What other concerns do you need to address in these six dimensions of health?

THE MATURING MARTIAL ARTIST

Consider the six dimensions of athletic health from an aging perspective. What do you need to do concerning each dimension in order to age as well as possible?

Strength: _____

Cardio: _____

Flexibility: _____

Nutrition: _____

Hydration: _____

Rest: _____

Other sources of information on the six dimensions of athletic health:

Other sources of information on aging:

Fightsheet 3

Dos and Dont's

DON'T IGNORE:

List all the injuries you know you have: _____

_____

List any other injuries that you think you may have or are in danger of sustaining: _____

_____

DO TREAT THE INJURY IMMEDIATELY:

NOTE: If you think your injury may need immediate medical attention then seek it at once.

• Does the injury need R.I.C.E. to reduce swelling?

R: Rest. What can you do to take the strain off the injury?

I: Ice. Ice pack or plastic bag filled with ice cubes. Put a cloth between ice and skin to protect from frostbite. Ice for 20 minutes on, 45 minutes off. Repeat several times a day.

C: Compression. How do you need to immobilize the injury? Does it need to be wrapped?

E: Elevation. How are you going to spend a lot of time with the injury elevated?

• Where will you sit or lie?

• What do you need to be comfortable while you keep the injury elevated?

• What do you need to keep within arm's reach so you can keep it elevated?

ICING LOG:

Date: _____ :Iced 20 minutes at (times)

Fightsheet 3a

DO IDENTIFY THE INJURY:

Identify the EXACT LOCATION(S) of injury.

- As best as you can tell, is the injury to a muscle, bone, joint, organ or other?

- What were you doing when the injury occurred?

- What makes it feel better?

- What makes it feel worse?

- Is there swelling or discoloration?

- Is this a chronic condition that is getting worse over time, or did it happen suddenly?

- Is there anything else that you can discern about your injury?

DON'T USE PAIN TO GAUGE INJURY OR HEALING:

Identify all locations of pain and rank the intensity of pain on a scale from one to 10.

(NOTE: This information is as much for your medical professionals as for yourself. Pain can mean any number of things medically and can provide your doctor with valuable information for proper diagnosis.)

DO SEEK PROFESSIONAL MEDICAL HELP:

Self-administered aid such as R.I.C.E. **HAS / HAS NOT** resulted in RAPID IMPROVEMENT (within 24 hours of injury).

- For chronic injury: How long has it been going on?

- What have you tried that hasn't resulted in healing?

- When are you going to seek professional medical attention? (Don't procrastinate, if you need it, do it!)

Initial appointment with doctor: _____

DON'T GIVE UP:

- Who are some people whose stories of overcoming adversity truly inspire you?

- Write down their names and where their stories can be found. You can revisit them any time you need an inspirational boost.

Fightsheet 4

Know Your Corner

What type of medical professionals do you need to see? (See page 34.)

CHOOSING A DOCTOR

- Doctor being considered (Name, address, phone #): _____

  _____

- Is the doctor **qualified**? (Initials after the name, what medical school did s/he graduate from, etc.)

- Is the doctor **specialized**? (Sports medicine, surgery, general practitioner, geriatrics, etc.) ☐ YES   ☐ NO

- Is s/he is a member of what organizations, especially in sports medicines? ☐ YES   ☐ NO   (See page 35.)

- Is s/he the team doctor for anyone, such as local high schools or colleges?

- Does s/he treat many athletes? ☐ YES   ☐ NO

- Is the doctor healthy, even **athletic**? ☐ YES   ☐ NO

- Is the doctor **empathetic** and understanding toward the plight of an injured athlete? ☐ YES   ☐ NO

- Is the doctor **interactive**? Will there be plenty of communication? ☐ YES   ☐ NO

- Is the doctor **comprehensive**? What types of treatments are available through his office? ☐ YES   ☐ NO

- Is the doctor **available**? ☐ YES   ☐ NO

- Is the doctor taking new patients? ☐ YES   ☐ NO

- Is the doctor covered by your insurance? ☐ YES   ☐ NO

- Is a referral by your primary care physician required from your insurance company? ☐ YES   ☐ NO

- Is the doctor affordable? ☐ YES   ☐ NO

- Is the doctor recommended? ☐ YES   ☐ NO

Local trainers, coaches and athletes you can ask about doctors:

    Whom did you ask?

    What was their response?

Research (especially on Internet): _____

Awards, articles in medical journals, lawsuits, etc.: _____

_____

First Choice of Medical Professional: _____

Name and office address and phone number: _____

_____

Second Choice: _____

Name and office address and phone number: _____

_____

DOCTOR'S VISITS:

    • Does the doctor allow tape recordings?

    • If not, will you take notes?

    • Will you take someone with you to help ask questions and remember what is said?

    • What issues, terminology, processes, etc. do you need to research to better communicate with the doctor?

IMPORTANT CONTACT INFORMATION:

Doctor: _____

Insurance company phone number: _____

Other medical professionals such as therapist, nutritionist, masseuse or chiropractor: _____

_____

Fightsheet 5

Redefine Your Goals

AFTER DOCTOR'S VISIT:

- What is the official diagnosis?

- What treatment methods have been prescribed?

- What medications are prescribed?

- What side effects should you watch out for?

- What is the projected timeline for recovery?

- What is the projected extent of recovery (100%, 75%, etc.)?

- What are the important actions that you will need to take to make the most of medical procedures, treatments and advice?

- What are some areas you need to research further?

- Where will you research your injury? (Internet, library, other)

- Anatomical research: Exactly what is injured, and how?
  In medical terminology: _____

  In plain English: _____

  - What tissues are involved?

  - What physical systems are affected?

  - What supporting systems are also affected?

  - What will the injury need in order to heal, and how does healing occur?

  - What terminology do you need to understand?

Recovery research:

What are the favored treatments for this type of injury?

- • Will there be rehabilitation involved?

- • Where will you get your therapy done?

- • How long will it take / how many sessions?

- • How much will your insurance cover?

- • What date do you expect to be released from doctor's care?

Useful Sources of Information (Web sites and books, for example):

Questions to ask next time you see your doctor:

Medical Log: _____ Date: _____

Who did you see? _____

Result of visit: _____

Changes to make in your routines: _____

_____

Therapy Sessions Log: _____ Date/Time: _____

Where and with whom? _____

When will your last one be? _____

What "homework" have your medical professionals given you to do? _____

☐ "I understand that ultimate responsibility for my health, healing and wellness lies with me."

Notes: _____

_____

_____

REDEFINE YOUR GOALS:

- What are some current goals that you are able to keep pursuing at this time?

- What are some current goals that you will have to set aside, at least for now?

- What are some new goals that you must set for yourself in order to attain optimum health and wellness?

PLAN:

Write a long list of everything you can begin doing now to proactively pursue the best health and healing you can attain. Answer questions such as:

- What other research can you begin?

- What actions can you take?

- What changes in lifestyle can you make starting now?

- What are the details of life that you will have to change?

- What are some things that you are going to do to keep the rest of you busy while your injured areas recover?

    Activities that do not involve your injured areas:_____

    Study/research: _____

    Entertainment: _____

    Other life pursuits: _____

    Other ideas to pass the time: _____

GOALS:

Break down your plans into specific and measurable goals.
(See Chapter 5 page 45 for an example.)

Recovery timeline: If given a clear date when you can expect to resume activity involving your injured areas, mark that date on your calendar. Do the same thing concerning when you might be able to add water exercises, weight-bearing exercises, aerobics, impact training and any other "milestones" that you would like to set as goals.

Fightsheet 6

Train Around an Injury

- Do you have clearance from your medical professionals to exercise?

- Will your insurance company pay your medical bills if you undo medical treatment by exercising?

- List the uninjured areas of your body that you need to work out as you "train around" your injured areas. List some basic exercises you can do for each one. (Refer to your Fightsheet 2: Six Dimensions and build on what you have listed there.)

- Now get creative. What other ways can you think of to get a good, overall workout for your uninjured areas and not place undue strain on your weakened and recovering injured areas?

- List the skills and techniques you can continue to train.

- List any skills from other martial arts disciplines you would like to work on while recovering such as joint locks, weapons, disarms, chokes and others.

- Warm-up and stretching: Appendix A on page 103 contains many exercises for range of motion and for the initial heating up of muscles prior to a workout. List those you can do while recovering.

Fightsheet 7

Posthab

DATE THAT YOU ARE CLEARED BY MEDICAL PERSONNEL TO RESUME NORMAL ACTIVITIES: _____

- How will you celebrate this victory?

- What new goals will you now set to take you from basically healed to a full-out martial arts workout?

CAUTION:

Consider factors or activities that could lead to re-injury and list them. What will you do to avoid them?

- What areas of your athleticism and body have atrophied significantly due to injury? (Examples include muscle mass, percentage of body fat, cardio and others.)

- What areas have probably compensated for the injured areas? (Examples include uninjured side versus injured side and strong legs versus weakened upper-body.)

- What are some issues that you need to be careful of in light of your answers to the previous questions?

- What skills and techniques have you lost proficiency in?

- What measures will you take to prevent yourself from overdoing your workouts and risking re-injury?

- What routines have you been doing recently that you feel you need to continue but perhaps with a bit more intensity? (Examples include adding light weights to range-of-motion exercises or adding burpees to your warm-up.)

POSTHAB WARM-UP

Visit Appendix A on page 103 for additional exercises to add to your warm-up routine.

Areas needing extra warm-up: _____

Exercises that target these areas: _____

POSTHAB AFFECTED AREA

• What cautions do you need to take to protect the newly recovered area?

• What exercise routines will you do to re-strengthen your recovering areas?

Strength: _____

Cardio: _____

Flexibility: _____

As you progress, how will you carefully "ramp up" your workout? Examples include:

• More reps or sets.
• More weight/resistance.
• More speed/explosiveness.

POSTHAB SUPPORTING AREAS

What exercise routines will you do to strengthen the healthy supporting areas around your recovering injured areas? For instance, a recovering knee needs a strong calf and quads.

Supporting area: _____

Exercises: _____

POSTHAB POSTURAL ALIGNMENT

• What exercises and routines will you add to strengthen and rebuild good posture and body alignment? Examples include using a Swiss ball and doing your kata/forms. (See Appendix A on page 103 for postural pointers and stretching exercises.)

POSTHAB AGILITY AND BALANCE

- What routines will you do to safely rebuild your sense of agility and balance? (Examples include using an agility ladder, Swiss ball, light plyometrics, standing on one foot and kata/forms.)

POSTHAB SKILLS AND TECHNIQUES

List the skills and techniques you need to begin carefully working on as well as the routines and exercises that will allow you to accomplish this without re-injury. _____

_____

POSTHAB PITFALLS

You know yourself better than anyone. Consider what issues you will probably struggle with during this transitional time. (Examples might include doing too much, tiring easily and quitting, lifting weights, cardio and regaining technique.)

PAIN

- Monitor your pain as you work out. Determine specifically what hurts, how badly and why.

- Determine if your pains are the "pains of excellence," such as soreness from your previous session, or a warning signal from your body of impending re-injury.

- How closely do you think it bears watching?

- If it doesn't clear up quickly, what are you going to do about it? Rather than ignore it or procrastinate, set a date for taking further action such as a visit to the doctor.

How can you adjust your workout regimen so that each element will give you multiple benefits?

What areas are in a serious "deficit" and need extra attention in order to catch up?

What compound or full-body exercises are needed to rebuild and strengthen the holistic connection between all your body parts? (Examples include burpees, tire flipping, plyometrics, shadowboxing, swimming and stand-up and ground-fighting drills.)

Fightsheet 8

Active Recovery

COOL DOWN:

- What cool down routines will you do after your workout session?

STRETCHING:

- What areas of stretching will you need to focus on after workout session? (See page 103 for examples)

HYDRATION:

- What will you use to replace water and electrolytes after your workout? (Examples include water and sports drinks.)

  Write down how much fluid you are determined to drink per day and after working out specifically.

ICE:

- What areas of your body will need icing, and what will you use to ice? Needs include commercial ice packs, plastic bags with ice cubes and water, cloth to prevent frostbite and bandages to hold ice on affected areas.

MASSAGE:

- If you are going to get a massage, when and where will you get it?

SHOWER:

- Will you need to take hot/cold/hot/cold showers after workout?

EPSOM SALTS:

- Can you take an Epsom salts bath (2 cups salt in the tub)?

NUTRITION:

- What proteins will you consume before and after the workout?

Amount:_____ Time:_____

- What carbohydrates will you consume after the workout?

Amount:_____ Time:_____

(See pages 18 and 69 for general guidelines.)

Fightsheet 9

Master Your Emotions

"I am a Martial Artist and QUITTING IS NOT AN OPTION."

Signature: _____ Date: _____

Consider your situation and what you are going through. Examine your journey through these seven emotions and ask yourself these important questions:

1 SHOCK

- Did you go through this emotion?
- Rate yourself on how you think you handled it.
- Have you had any relapses?
- Are you honestly past this stage yet?
- If yes, are you celebrating this progress?
- If not, what triggers this emotion in your mind?
- What do you need in order to work your way through this emotion and move on?

2 DENIAL

- Did you go through this emotion?
- Rate yourself on how you think you handled it.
- Have you had any relapses?
- Are you honestly past this stage yet?
- If yes, are you celebrating your progress?
- If not, what triggers this emotion in your mind?
- What do you need in order to work your way through this emotion and move on?

3 ANGER

- Did you go through this emotion?
- Rate yourself on how you think you handled it.
- Have you had any relapses?
- Are you honestly past this stage yet?
- If yes, are you celebrating your progress?
- If not, what triggers this emotion in your mind?
- What do you need in order to work your way through this emotion and move on?

4 BARGAINING

- Did you go through this emotion?
- Rate yourself on how you think you handled it.
- Have you had any relapses?
- Are you honestly past this stage yet?
- If yes, are you celebrating your progress?

- If not, what triggers this emotion in your mind?
- What do you need in order to work your way through this emotion and move on?

5 DEPRESSION

- Did you go through this emotion?
- Rate yourself on how you think you handled it.
- Have you had any relapses?
- Are you honestly past this stage yet?
- If yes, are you celebrating your progress?
- If not, what triggers this emotion in your mind?
- What do you need in order to work your way through this emotion and move on? (There is more about depression on page 76.)

6 TESTING

- Did you go through this emotion?
- Rate yourself on how you think you handled it.
- Have you had any relapses?
- Are you honestly past this stage yet?
- If yes, are you celebrating your progress?
- If not, what triggers this emotion in your mind?
- What do you need in order to work your way through this emotion and move on?

7 ACCEPTANCE

- Have you honestly arrived here?
- Rate yourself on how you think you handled the journey overall.
- Have you had any relapses?
- If so, which emotions do you sometimes still struggle with?
- Can you think of ways to concentrate on getting completely past these relapses?
- What do you need in order to work your way through these relapses so you can stay in the stable mind-set of Acceptance and move on?

IDENTIFY DEPRESSION:

See the checklist for signs of depression on page 77 and examine yourself. If you are suffering from depression, it needs to be addressed by medical professionals. Don't hesitate; see your doctor.

ENDORPHINS:

- What can you do to get your heart rate up for at least 20 minutes so that your body will begin releasing mood-elevating, pain-reducing endorphins?

Test yourself and determine how long it takes for your endorphins to kick in and make you feel better.

RECOVERY TIME:

Looking at a long total recovery time can be depressing so break it into smaller pieces. Set a realistic goal and date for each stage of your recovery such as completing therapy sessions, getting your doctor's release, first day back in the gym and others, then focus on achieving one goal at a time.

Goal One and Target Date: _____

Goal Two and Target Date: _____

Goal Three and Target Date: _____

Goal Four and Target Date: _____

Goal Five and Target Date: _____

FINANCES:

Don't let depression cause you to neglect this area of your life; it will only make things worse. Schedule a time (once a week, for example) when you will take care of your financial life.

Focus on Finances Day/Times: _____

BODILY FUNCTIONS:

- If you need someone to help you personally, who will it be?

- What are you going to do for them to show your appreciation?

SELF-DOUBT:

If depression causes you to do some soul-searching, turn that into a positive by thinking these issues through and settling some conclusions about who you are and what you want in life.

Write these things down in a private journal, including the date. Being able to "dump" it all down somewhere and put it away can be helpful.

Work diligently through the next section on Positive Mental Attitude.

LAUGH:

List those things that usually make you laugh and bring joy into your life, and schedule them into your week.

It will be fun to: _____ Date: _____

It will be fun to: _____ Date: _____

It will be fun to: _____ Date: _____

OTHER AREAS OF LIFE:

- What other areas of your life are being affected by depression, and what can you do to counteract it?

    Area of life affected: _____

    How depression is affecting me: _____

    Actions I can take to counteract it:_____

POSITIVE MENTAL ATTITUDE:

List the good things that you are purposefully putting into your mind—things that are inspiring, motivating, positive, educational or relaxing.

- What can you add to this list and put into your mind on a daily basis?

- What are the bad things you are putting into your mind? (Examples are negativity, blame, anger, depression or fear.)

• What actions can you take to stop putting that into your mind and replace it with the good stuff?

Answer the following questions in as positive a manner as you can:

• What do you think is going to happen to you?

• What do you think you are going to accomplish through this time in your life?

• What do you believe the future holds for you?

• How much faith do you have in your ability to recover?

• Who inspires you with their own story?

• What books, magazines, movies and other things fill you with inspiration?

• Do you have them? Where can you get them?

• What inspirational stories do others recommend?

• How have you progressed and how does it inspire/encourage you?

• How can you use your own story to help inspire others?

Fightsheet 10

From Vision to Reality

VISION:

Vision is "a clear mental image of a preferable future." If you haven't already, write out your personal vision of what you want your future to be like.

Read your vision at least once every day, imagining how it will be when it becomes real.

Find pictures that represent to you your preferred future and post them around where you will see them often. Date done:_____

VISUALIZATION:

- Following the guidelines on page 86, construct in your imagination a visualization scenario about your specific needs for optimal healing. Remember to include intelligence, imagination and emotion.

- Make it like a movie, and begin each visualization session by imagining yourself going to a movie theatre, sitting in your seat and waiting for the movie to begin.

- Write down the elements you want to include and the specific actions you want your body to take. (Examples might include healing in a specific area, your optimism and enthusiasm, or calcium being laid into a fractured bone.)

- Run your inner-movie visualization at least twice a day: once in the afternoon when you have a personal quiet time and again just before you go to sleep.

- Keep a log of visualization sessions, remembering the importance of building a habit.

- Write out the noticeable differences that visualization makes in your recovery and mental state.

- Elements and specifics of my visualization:

- Visualization log: Date/Time:

- Noticeable benefits of visualization:

ICONS

Following the information on page 91, select a couple of things to act as daily icons for your healing progress and goals.

My icon is: _____

It represents: _____

This is what I will do to interact with it: _____

I AM STATEMENTS

You already have pictures, words and self-coaching working to your advantage. Now add "I am" statements to your self-talk. An "I am" statement is a positively stated fact about who you are or want to be. Examples might be: "I am healing well." "I am optimistic about the future." "I am making daily progress toward my important goals."

Write out as many as you can think of, then read aloud the most meaningful 20 or 30 at least once each day. Log your progress for at least two weeks.

"I am" statement log: _____

Date: _____

HELP FROM OTHERS

(See page 92.)

Authorities that help me be persistent:

Names: _____

Helps me by: _____

Peers that help me be persistent:

Names: _____

Helps me by: _____

People who hinder my persistence and positive progress, and how I will avoid them:

_____

_____

REMEMBER:

PERSISTENCE is the only way to victory.

PERSISTENCE is the opposite of QUITTING.

The KEY to PERSISTENCE is DESIRE.

- What are doing to maintain the passionate fire of DESIRE?

- What can you do to build more of that in your life? Be specific.

- What is hindering your passionate desire and working against you?

- What can you do to erect barriers against these hindrances in your life?

Fightsheet 11

When You Can't Come Back

Will you be a martial artist for the rest of your life?_____

Reminder: Accepting change is not the same as accepting defeat.

Take an honest, hard look at your life. What changes are permanent and out of your hands?

Have you accepted these changes? If not, what can you do to move forward?

Permanent change: _____

I have/have not accepted this change. _____

To move forward, I can: _____

Role models for my future career in the martial arts include:_____

_____

Things I would consider for my future career in the martial arts. (See pages 97 to 98 for examples.)

By now you are probably pretty good at making plans, setting goals and seeing them through. Begin that process now concerning your long-range career in the martial arts. Ask yourself questions such as: Who do I want to be? What do I want to achieve? What do I want to be doing the rest of my life? Where can I begin gathering information about how to get from here to there? Who do I know who has already done it (or something similar)? Start the planning process today and give yourself plenty of time.

Note: Many of the strategies and techniques described in this book will work for many kinds of goals and achievements, not just injury recovery. Remember, the sky is the limit and the possibilities are endless.

Write an honest, believable and measurable description of what you hope to be able to do as a martial artist five and 10 years from now. _____

What goals would you like to set for inner-growth and life development as your body ages?

_____

Write down any other goals that will require several years to attain. _____

_____

Fightsheet 12

Celebrate

Many times in the text and Fightsheets you have been encouraged to celebrate any and all accomplishments. This not only reinforces good activities and habits but also gives you something to look forward to and builds optimism and your positive mental attitude. It also builds a spirit of gratitude and hinders a spirit of negativity and depression.

Here is a way for you to record your victories and how you will celebrate them. Check them off or highlight them as you achieve them.

When I accomplish: _____

I will celebrate by: _____

Date I plan to do this: _____

This injury and recovery experience has made me a better person in these ways: __

_____

Greatest life lessons I've learned through this experience: _____

_____

Your final determination revisited from Fightsheet 1:

Make this PROMISE TO YOURSELF, and post a copy of it where you will see it often.

> *I am a fighter and I am going to achieve optimal health and wellness to the best of my ability.*
>
> *I WILL: Take responsibility for my health, healing and wellness.*
>
> *I WILL: Carry out my customized, comprehensive plan as laid out in my Fightsheets.*
>
> *I WILL: Carry out this plan in a holistic manner.*
>
> *I WILL: Develop the heart of a champion.*

Signature: _____ Date: _____

Are you ready?

ARE YOU READY?

FIGHT!